Inflection Journal
Volume 12 - LOVE
December 2025

Inflection acknowledges the Wurundjeri Woi Wurrung People of the Kulin Nation, the Traditional Custodians of the land on which we live and work and on which the contents of this journal were assembled and published. We pay our respects to Indigenous Elders past and present and to emerging Aboriginal voices.

Sovereignty was never ceded.

Inflection is published annually by the Melbourne School of Design at the University of Melbourne and Melbourne Books.

Editors: Sunny Brearley, Sivan Danin, Alec Gutteridge, Lachie Meckiff, Charlotte Schaller, Nethuni Sumanaweera and Dorothea Yannoulidis

Collaborators: Maximilian Bufardeci (Logo), John Martin (Sub-Editor)

Academic Advisor: Dr. AnnMarie Brennan

The editors would like to thank all those involved in the production of this journal for their generous assistance and support.

A special acknowledgement is due to Dr AnnMarie Brennan, whose continual work across the development of Inflection has been invaluable; to David Tenenbaum of Melbourne Books for his tireless help and support; and to Professor Donald Bates, whose generosity has ensured this volume reaches the printing press.

For editorial enquiries contact:
editorial@inflectionjournal.com

For sales enquiries contact:
info@melbournebooks.com.au

inflectionjournal.com
@inflectionjournal

ISSN 2199-8094

ISBN 9781922779571

Melbourne Books
Level 9, 100 Collins Street,
Melbourne, VIC 3000,
Australia
www.melbournebooks.com.au
info@melbournebooks.com.au

Cover image:
Untitled #52 - Archive of Longing Series
© Ali Tahayori

Back cover image:
Untitled #16 - Archive of Longing Series
© Ali Tahayori

Inside cover image:
Untitled #46 - Archive of Longing Series
© Ali Tahayori

Ali Tahayori is an interdisciplinary artist born in Shiraz, Iran, currently living and working in Sydney, Australia, on Gadigal Country. Translating the traditional Iranian craft of Aine-Kari (Mirror-Works) into a contemporary visual vocabulary, his practice combines a discourse about diaspora and displacement with an exploration of queerness—in both cases, poignantly testifying to his experience of being othered. He has exhibited locally and internationally and has been a finalist and winner of several local and international art prizes. Tahayori is represented by THIS IS NO FANTASY Gallery in Melbourne.

THE UNIVERSITY OF MELBOURNE | msd Melbourne School of Design | FACULTY OF ARCHITECTURE, BUILDING AND PLANNING www.msd.unimelb.edu.au

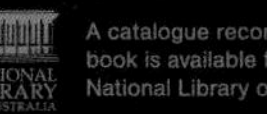

A catalogue record for this book is available from the National Library of Australia

CONTRIBUTORS

Tony Birch
Tony Birch holds the Boisbouvier Chair in Australian Literature at the University of Melbourne. In 2017 he was awarded the Patrick White prize, in recognition of his contribution to Australian literature. He is the author of four novels, five short fiction collections and two poetry books. In 2022 his book, *Dark as Last Night* was awarded the Christina Stead Literary Prize and the Steele Rudd Literary Award. The book was also shortlisted for the 2022 Prime Minister's Literary Award for fiction. His most recent book is *On Kim Scott: Writers on Writers* (2024).

Simona Castricum
Simona Castricum is an artist working on Wurundjeri Country in Naarm/Melbourne, exploring trans and queer spatial politics through music, architecture and design. Simona's collaborative, mentoring practice spans performance, broadcasting, installation and writing—imagining future worlds through sonic and spatial propositions grounded in autofiction and transfeminist practice. She is a recipient of the University of Melbourne Chancellor Award for her doctoral research, "What if Safety Becomes Permanent? Architecture and Music as a Site of Transing." Simona is the inaugural winner of the Australian Institute of Architects' Gender Equity and Diversity Award in Victoria.

Vinu Daniel
Vinu Daniel is the founder of Wallmakers, an award-winning architecture practice specialising in sustainable, cost-effective and context-sensitive design. He earned his BArch from the College of Engineering, Trivandrum in 2005 following which he worked with the Auroville Earth Institute for the United Nations Development Programme on post-tsunami reconstruction. Since founding Wallmakers in 2007, he has pioneered innovative techniques like the Debris Wall and Shuttered Debris Wall, using site-sourced and waste materials. Wallmakers has received global recognition, including the Royal Academy Dorfman Award (2022) and a TED Talk invitation

Celeste De Clario Davis
Celeste de Clario Davis is a Melbourne-based filmmaker and artist, working across video and photography. Her practice explores the epistemic and representational dimensions of lens-based documentation, specifically in relation to events, spaces and objects that are in flux, or unstable. Most recently, she completed her first Screen Australia-funded feature documentary, *Things Will Be Different* (2023) with Lucie McMahon.

Fatou Kiné Dieye
Fatou Kiné Dieye is a consultant specialised in the design of buildings, policy frameworks and the corresponding supply chain mechanics necessary for building Sub-Saharan Africa's next generation of green and inclusive cities. She was previously the Managing Director of Skat Consulting's offices in Rwanda, Burundi and DR Congo, responsible for the implementation of the Swiss Cooperation's construction industry transformation program for Africa's Great Lakes Region. Prior to joining Skat, Fatou was team leader for the Affordable Housing and Neighborhood Development Unit for the City of Kigali and an urban designer for the New York City Department of City Planning. Fatou holds degrees in architecture, urban planning and sustainability management from Princeton and Columbia Universities.

Garry Emery
Garry Emery established one of the most influential design practices in Australia. He is a design consultant for high-profile national and international projects, including the world's three tallest buildings. He has lectured, been widely published, received numerous awards and has exhibited globally. He has served on international juries for design and national juries for architecture and urbanism. He is a member of Alliance Graphique International; a fellow of the Society of Experiential Design; a fellow of the Australian Institute of Architects; a fellow of the Chicago Athenaeum Museum of Architecture and Design; and a fellow of the International Council of Design. He holds a PhD in Design from RMIT University, where he is an Adjunct Professor.

Thomas Essex Plath
Thomas Essex Plath is an architectural practitioner, who teaches and occasionally writes about architecture. He has a background in both architecture and sociology. His practice, teaching and writing focus on housing and domestic life. He has worked on large-scale social housing projects in Australia and the Netherlands. He is currently undertaking research on contemporary apartment floor plans in Melbourne, alongside writing on the everyday in architecture.

Hélène Frichot
Hélène Frichot is currently Professor of Architecture and Philosophy, Faculty of Architecture, Building and Planning, University of Melbourne, Australia. Previously, she was Professor of Critical Studies and Gender Theory and Director of Critical Studies in Architecture, KTH Stockholm, Sweden. Her recent publications include *Dirty Theory* (2019) and *Creative Ecologies* (2018) and the co-edited collections *Infrastructural Love: Caring for our Architectural Support Systems* (2022); *Architectural Affects After Deleuze and Guattari* (2021); *Writing Architectures* (2020); a special issue of the *Journal of Architecture, Jennifer Bloomer: A Revisitation* (2024); and a special issue of the *Deleuze and Guattari Studies Journal*, celebrating 100 years since Gilles Deleuze's birth, entitled *A Deleuzian Life—A People to Come* (2025).

Felix Garner Davis & Nina Nervegna
Felix Garner Davis and Nina Nervegna are designers and writers. They collaborate across architectural practice and transdisciplinary speculation, focusing on small civic buildings and sites around Naarm/Melbourne. Their approach fuses traditional and experimental methods, equally interested in construction detailing, poetry, counter-cartography, field recording and installation. Before studying architecture, Felix trained in literary studies, specialising in spatial poetics and Nina trained in fine art and service design, specialising in painting and wayfinding. Their graduate thesis at the Melbourne School of Design "Limb" received the Bates Smart Award. Nina also received the Ernest Fooks Memorial Award and the Edward Fielder Billson Medal.

Lina Ghotmeh
Lebanese-born Lina Ghotmeh, founder of Lina Ghotmeh—Architecture, is celebrated for her sustainable, innovative and inclusive designs. Guided by her philosophy, 'Archaeology of the Future,' her work connects history, nature and materiality. Her notable projects include the redesign of the Western Range galleries of the British Museum; Qatar's permanent pavilion at the Venice Biennale, Bahrain Pavilion for Expo 2025; the 22nd Serpentine Pavilion in London (2023); and the Estonian National Museum in Tartu (2016). Lina Ghotmeh lectures internationally and has held leading academic roles at Yale University, the University of Toronto and Harvard University Graduate School of Design. Her awards include the 2023 Great Arab Minds Award, the 2020 Schelling Architecture Award and the French Architecture Académie's Prix Dejean (2016).

Greg Girard
Greg Girard is a Canadian photographer whose work has examined the social and physical transformations across Asia's biggest cities for more than four decades. He is the author of numerous photographic books, including *City of Darkness: Life in Kowloon Walled City; Snack Sakura; American Stopover; JAL 76-88; Tokyo-Yokosuka 1976-1983; Hotel Okinawa; Under Vancouver 1972-1982; Hanoi Calling; In the Near Distance;* and *Phantom Shanghai*. His work is held in the collection of M+ Museum, Hong Kong; the National Gallery of Canada; the Art Gallery of Ontario; the Vancouver Art Gallery; and other public and private collections.

Bradley Kerr
Bradley Kerr is a Quandamooka man and architect on Wurundjeri Country. He is an Associate Lecturer at the University of Sydney and Monash University. He co-chairs the Australian Institute of Architects' First Nations Advisory Committee, contributes to boards and committees, curates the BLAKitecture series. He was awarded the 2024 Victorian Emerging Architect Prize and 2023 Dulux Study Prize.

Kaylie Salvatori
Kaylie Salvatori is a Salt-Water Yuin woman and the Founding Director of COLA Studio. She is a landscape architect and a cultural design strategist who specialises in Indigenous design collaboration and Country-positive approaches. She priorities Country in her work, advocating for First Peoples' custodianship. She connects cultural-ecological systems in public and commercial spaces, excelling in concept ideation, storytelling and material selection while promoting biodiversity through her unique design practices.

Jimenez Lai
Jimenez Lai was born in Taiwan, came of age in Canada and lives in Los Angeles. Before establishing Bureau Spectacular, Lai lived in a desert shelter at Taliesin and resided in a shipping container at Atelier Van Lieshout on the piers of Rotterdam. His first book, *Citizens of No Place: An Architectural Graphic Novel* (2012) was published by Princeton Architectural Press with a grant from the Graham Foundation. Lai represented Taiwan at the 14th Venice Architecture Biennale and his work is held in the permanent collection of MoMA, SFMOMA, Art Institute of Chicago and LACMA.

Iggy Licup
Iggy Licup is a Filipino design practitioner based in Melbourne. A graduate of the University of Melbourne with a MArch, his work explores the theoretical and practical possibilities of design representation, as well as personal themes at the intersection of immigrant identity and queerness. With a goal to 'multi-disciplinise' his current practice, he is furthering his academic pursuits through an MA in Arts Management at RMIT University.

Samiha Meem
Samiha Meem is a designer and writer whose research explores how image, media infrastructures and popular culture intersect with the representation, consumption and production of architecture. Her writing has appeared in *e-flux Architecture*, *Real Review* and the *Journal for Architectural Education*. Her design work and collaborations have been exhibited at Nuit Blanche Toronto, La Centrale galerie Powerhouse and Nike Soho and featured in *New York Magazine*, *Interview Magazine* and the *Architect's Newspaper*. She teaches architecture at the Knowlton School at The Ohio State University, following her 2023–25 Howard E. LeFevre '29 Emerging Practitioner Fellowship. She previously taught at McGill University, where she earned her MArch and holds a BArch from the University of Waterloo.

Jane Mooney
Jane Mooney's professional status was first established at Emerystudio, then in London with Pentagram, a renowned global practice. An award-winning multidisciplinary designer, she is a pedant with a focus on communications and a lifetime passion for art, architecture and design. With Garry Emery she is a communications and brand design consultant for the Venice Virtual Biennale of Architecture. Much of her work dedicated to cultural enterprises, particularly within the visual arts and architectural sectors. She holds a BArch (Hons) in Graphic Design from Swinburne University of Technology.

Nervegna Reed Architects
Nervegna Reed Architecture is an award-winning architecture practice established by Anna Nervegna and Toby Reed in 2004. NR projects include social housing and community projects in regional Victoria, Melbourne, Hobart and urban planning in China. Their design for the Central Goldfields Art Gallery was exhibited in the 2023 Venice Architecture Biennale, won the RAIA's John George Knight Award for Heritage Architecturean award for the best public building category at the 2A Awards in Dubai. They extend their architectural dialogue with writing and the making of architectural documentaries and videos. NR have guest edited *2A Magazine* and *Architecture Victoria*. Toby contributed the chapter 'Screenness' to the book *The Physical and the Digital City* (2024).

Alberto Pérez-Gómez
Alberto Pérez-Gómez studied architecture and practiced in Mexico City. In 1983 he became the Director of Carleton University's School of Architecture (Ottawa, Canada). Since 1987 he occupied the Bronfman Chair at McGill University, where he founded the History and Theory post-graduate programs and is now Emeritus Professor. He was recognized with the Order of Canada in 2020. Pérez-Gómez is the author of numerous essays published worldwide. His books include *Architecture and the Crisis of Modern Science* (1983; Hitchcock Award in 1984), *Polyphilo* (1992), *Architectural Representation and the Perspective Hinge* (1997), *Built upon Love* (2006), *Attunement* (2016), *Timely Meditations*, (2016) and *An Alliterative Lexicon of Architectural Memories* (2024).

Sarah Robinson
Sarah Robinson is an architect, writer and educator. She was the founding president of the Frank Lloyd Wright School of Architecture Board of Governors. Her books—*The Architecture of Resonance: from Objects to Interactions* (2025) *Architecture Is a Verb* (2021), *Mind in Architecture: Embodiment, Neuroscience and the Future of Design* with Juhani Pallasmaa (2015) and *Nesting: Body, Dwelling, Mind* (2011)—are among the first to explore the connections between the embodied cognitive sciences and architecture. She is a is an Adjunct Professor at Aalborg University, Denmark and teaches the Neuroscience Applied to Architectural Design program at IUAV University of Venice, where she also serves on the scientific board.

Alex Selenitsch
Alex Selenitsch is a Melbourne-based poet and architect known primarily for his concrete poems but also for his drawings, artists books, objects, furniture and architecture. An exhibition of his architectural research, titled 'Language Factory,' was held in the DULUX Gallery, Melbourne School of Design, during the COVID lockdown. His most recent books are *LOOK!* (2021) a collection of his concrete poems; and *Purgatorio Re-placed* (2021), a re-write of Dante's *Purgatorio*.

Robyn Sweeney
Robyn Sweaney is an artist working and living in Murwillumbah, northern NSW. Her practice excavates the complexities of place by responding to the suburban mundane of Australian environments. Her tightly refined work in acrylic, gouache and graphite is inspired by her local landscape and many road trips throughout rural Australia over the past 20 years. Sweaney's work is in the State Library of New South Wales collection, Artbank and in numerous other regional galleries and private collections throughout Australia and Europe. She has exhibited widely as a solo artist and as part of many selected prize and collaborative exhibitions.

James Urlini
James Urlini is interested in how heritage values are interpreted and shared through public history and microhistory, with a focus on postwar migrant and industrial heritage. Outside of research, he works as a graphic designer at Arcitecta, a Northcote-based database management software company, where he contributes to the development of a digital asset management system (DAMS) for research, media and entertainment and cultural institutions. He holds a MArch/MUCH from the University of Melbourne.

William Ward
William Ward is an Education Fellow in Architectural History & Theory at the Melbourne School of Design. His research areas include scholarship of teaching and learning (SoTL) in architecture and design, more-than-human design and interdisciplinary design pedagogy. In particular, he is interested in how emerging models of design practice and education might support sustainable, just and inclusive futures. He holds a MArch from the University of Melbourne.

CONTENTS

EDITORIAL

LOVE AND ITS INCARNATES

Alec Gutteridge, Charlotte Schaller & Dorothea Yannoulidis

In Bertrand Russell's *Has Man a Future* (1961), the author imagines himself as a character in the Egyptian *Book of the Dead* (ca. 1550–50 BCE).[1] He stands before Osiris, Judge of the Underworld, offering a justification for humanity's cruelty and endless pursuit of power, begging for clemency on the world's behalf. He speaks of love—not between individuals, but a love that embraces the earth and all of humanity. For Russell, love was the redeeming force that might secure the future from the looming threat of apocalypse brought about by the nuclear age. He pleads: "Lord, Osiris, we beseech Thee to grant us a respite, and a chance to emerge from ancient folly into a world of light and love and loveliness."[2]

In the same way today, man-made catastrophes such as climate change, inequality and global instability pose similar threats to humanity's future; we are beset by those same ancient follies. Given that the prospect of judgement remains unsettled, this volume of *Inflection* engages with Russell's assertion that love might save us all—and suggests that it may also make us better designers.

Love is rarely addressed within architectural discourse. The subject is perhaps regarded as too trivial or intangible for serious academic attention. However, the way we love and think about love may be understood as a palimpsest, on whose surface is etched the sum of what we value and believe. Each revision leaves behind a faint indentation in our collective imagination, as one set of values is swept aside by its antecedents. In this way, the analysis of love can tell us much about who we are and where we have come from. To reflect upon love is to reflect upon the human condition, upon why we create and what we value. It is a necessary consideration in design, one that we believe may help us in dealing with the wicked problems that we, as a society, now face.[3]

We tend to imagine we know what love is, or that we can recognise it in ourselves. In *All About Love* (1999), bell hooks describes love, not in popular depictions of devotion or betrayal, but as a structure to live by. It is a 'love ethic,' a system of mutualism, care and fraternity, built and maintained between people and that, in turn, looks after them as well.

This volume is concerned with how we might, as designers and creators, contribute to a world that "pre-supposes that everyone has [the] right to be free, to live fully and well [...] wherein we see our lives and our fate as intimately connected to those of everyone on the planet."[4] In this way, it suggests that love might provide the key to a more connected future.

What of our personal relationship to love? During the collation of this volume, the Australian Centre for Contemporary Art (ACCA) announced the exhibition: *Five Acts of Love*. To us, this was timely—an artistic exploration of our same quest to understand the power of love. Amongst its artists, Ali Tahayori, whose series *Archive of Longing* graces the covers of this volume, visualises a desperate search for love in old family photos. To Tahayori, these are places where love is, at first glance, not apparent. Hands holding, legs touching and arms over shoulders become enlarged, represented as small clues illustrative of a much larger phenomenon: the embodied, manifest qualities of love. The fragile trust that is necessary for love is crystalline in the anxious embraces of Tahayori's subjects. They are both bound and held by one another, reflecting the most profound of human feelings.

Through the lens of care, problems within architectural practice and pedagogy become visible. The stymieing effects of the corporate university, extractive industry practices and the rapidly shrinking purview of the architect are amongst them. How might new models for architectural output be created that do not result in such widespread dissatisfaction? Why is architectural education moving to align more rigidly with an increasingly irrelevant and failing industry? Why not try a system of education that places more emphasis upon nurturing students' development?

Now more than ever, it seems harder to convince our institutions that any systems require nurturing or maintaining, as the logic of the market dominates our cultural sphere. *Meanjin*, a cultural touchstone and Australia's longest-running literary journal, has seen its funding cut and after publishing for 85 years, it will cease to do so at the end of this one. In 1940, Clem Christensen introduced the first issue with the quote: "Literature and art, poetry and drama do not spring into being at the word of command. Their life is a continuous process growing within itself, and its suppression is death."[5]

All around us, we can see calls for the systems within which we exist to be nurtured and to nurture us. For these systems to be more thoroughly understood by those who administer them so they might serve us better. Instead, public housing projects are set for demolition across Melbourne, whilst public-private partnerships obscure the destruction of our social safety nets behind bland policy designations like community housing or tenancy blindness. The problems we face call for systems that care and that nurture and value the links between us. The challenge becomes designing those systems. We see various examples of this way of thinking throughout this volume, whether it be through consideration of the urban infrastructure of Kigali or reflections on the psychic landscapes through which we travel in our childhood neighbourhoods. Our relationships are the sum of us and those relationships must be understood.

For Russell, love is only possible once we have dragged ourselves from "the morass of ancient ignorance."[6] Today, the indictments of our species continue to accumulate. In Palestine, Sudan, the United States and elsewhere in the world, atrocities are committed by those in the thralls of power. The pursuit of power remains an *ignis fatuus*—a deceptive light, enticing us to return to the morass.

In a creative discipline that, more than any other, requires the consent of power for its inception and in an industry that contributes to more than 40 percent of global greenhouse emissions, it is vital that designers recognise the significance of the ethic by which we design and that

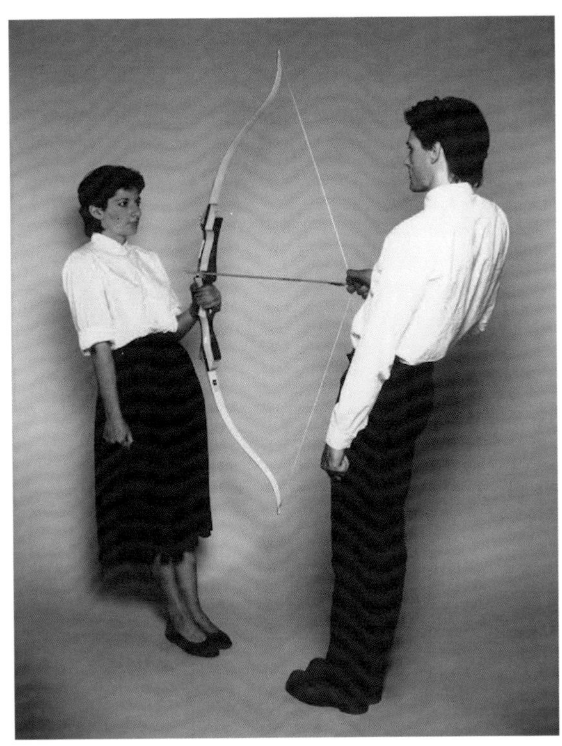

Above: Marina Abramović and Ulay, *Rest Energy*, 1980, image courtesy of Marina Abramovic and Sean Kelly Gallery.

we interrogate the assumptions about our discipline.[7] We must understand that the modes of production which we have inherited are malleable and perhaps in need of change. Systems that put people first and recognise our shared fate are necessary and have the potential to contribute to our collective salvation. We must persist, as love, in all its incarnations, remains worthy of preservation.

We would like to acknowledge the generosity of all our contributors—artists, architects, writers, students and designers who have devoted their time and ideas to the making of this volume. Without their inputs this publication would not have been possible.

01 Bertrand Russell, *Has Man a Future?* (London: Penguin Books, 1961), 14.
02 Russell, *Has Man a Future?*, 14.
03 Horst W. J. Rittel and Melvin M. Webber, "Dilemmas in a General Theory of Planning," *Policy Sciences* 4, no. 2 (1973): 155–169.
04 bell hooks, *All About Love: New Visions* (New York: William Morrow, 1999), 87.
05 "First Issue Editorial." *Meanjin*, December 29, 1940. https://meanjin.com.au/essays/first-issue-editorial/.
06 Russell, *Has Man a Future?*, 16.
07 United Nations Environment Programme. "Building Materials and the Climate: Constructing a New Future." UNEP – UN Environment Programme, September 12, 2023.

TRAM-TRACK DREAMING

Tony Birch

The interconnection between place and memory is central to not only my writing but how I exist in the world. I carry histories of street corners, the walls of factory buildings, houses and vacant blocks of land; some real, some destroyed by progress, others imagined, reaching back to a time six decades ago and more. In recent years the recovery of 'ghost signs,' faded advertising stencils on the side of buildings, has fed our nostalgia for idealised homelife and Robur Tea. I hold ghost memories in my body, an archive of my own past. Dormant images, emotions, events and fractured conversations, are often triggered by my interaction with the performance of daily life.

Recently I decided to walk from my home into the city, which I often do. I avoid the main thoroughfares, preferring to criss-cross the streets and lanes of gridded inner Melbourne. Although I'm a wanderer, I also have prescribed rituals, places I need to walk by and through to reassure myself that I'm grounded. For instance, anytime I head from Fitzroy to the top end of Bourke Street I choose the same route I've taken since I was a child.

The pocket-shaped park on the corner of Albert and Spring Streets, close to the State Parliament, provides a sanctuary for me. I don't know the name of the park and I'll choose now to not disturb my ignorant bliss by 'googling' to discover the relevant information. In fact, I'd encourage walkers of the city to avoid digital information, including maps, wherever possible. The beauty of an urban walk is in the unknown. Getting lost itself is a treasure not to be missed.

When I walk through the small pocket parkland, at some point a memory, most often from my childhood, will visit me. It is this park that I'd I walked through when heading to the movies as a kid. I was in the park only a few months ago when I spotted my childhood self a little ahead of me on the path. I was holding hands with my older sister. We had been to the Regent Theatre in Collins Street that day and had seen the movie *Planet of the Apes*. The film so excited us that we talked about it all the way home.

A block away from 'Pocket Park,' as I've just titled it, is the Carlton Gardens, or as we knew it as children, the 'Exhibition Gardens,' in honour of the grand nineteenth century building housed within its grounds. When I was a small boy I swam at a pond that used to be in the middle of the gardens, with my brothers, sisters and cousins. Many years ago, a playground was built over the top of the pond. Whenever I walk by the playground, the screams of enjoyment from kids playing on the swings remain as they were sixty years ago. All that's missing is the water.

Unfortunately, my strongest ghost memory of this place is not one of children, of us enjoying a day out. What I remember so clearly in this place is the day when I discovered my mother, sheltered behind a tree, deep in conversation with her younger sister, my godmother. I eavesdropped on their whispers that afternoon and wish to this day that I hadn't done so. I heard my auntie tell my mother that she was sick and that she would soon die. My mother looked across at me and ordered me to return to the water and play with my three young cousins, my auntie's children.

Over the past year or more, debate has raged over the proposed demolition of the public housing high-rise towers that dominate the skyline in inner-city suburbs including Richmond, Collingwood, Carlton, North Melbourne and Fitzroy. The slum reclamation program that created the towers was born from a propagandist campaign first initiated in the 1930s, a lie that demonised communities of the inner-city for the next fifty years. It is only in unethical fiction that a woman residing in 'Little George Street, Fitzroy' in 1935, could ever be described as an 'inferior harlot,' in order that she would serve the singular purpose of justifying the destruction of entire communities.

The irony of labelling women as the personification of urban evil, is cruel on many levels. The success of urban planners in the postwar period was such that many women and the families and communities they supported lost their homes, streets and social connection. The high-rise estates, supposedly built to eradicate this seeming menace, barely enjoyed a honeymoon period themselves. It is not surprising that within months of Fitzroy's Atherton Gardens public housing estate opening in 1970, that a headline appeared in one of Melbourne's daily newspapers describing Atherton Gardens as a 'High-Rise Hell.'

I lived in Fitzroy as a child and was privileged to be a member of six households of extended family living on two neighbouring streets. The destruction of my childhood community was violent and near complete. I live in the suburb today and enjoy walking the street and lanes taking photographs. During my walks, I often feel I have no more insight into the suburb's past than more recent arrivals. My childhood memories of Fitzroy come to life at a moment of their choosing, not mine. A switch occurs, a door is opened and I can see and feel my past self.

We walk the streets of the city both innocent of the past and deeply embedded in it. Even visitors to a city they have never walked before are implicated, for better or worse. Melbourne is a colonial city built on stolen Aboriginal Wurundjeri Country. The history of this city is a story of dispossession and each of us are part of this story, just as each of us are responsible for recognising this history. When I walk the streets of this city, I welcome the responsibility offered to me by Aboriginal people.

I was on one of my regular walks recently when I cut through the dreaded Little George Street into Napier. It was a weekday morning, only a few minutes before the first bell rang out at the nearby George Street state school, my father's childhood school. I quickly became entangled in a procession marching out of the Atherton Gardens public housing estate. I was amongst school children, their friends and parents. Most, if not all of the children and their families are refugees from the African continent. While some of the kids walked quietly holding a parent's hand, most began playing on the street, hugging their friends and patting dogs in the nearby park.

I had two thoughts during this experience. The first was one of anger. Watching the children, who were so happy and their parents both mildly scolding and smiling at their kids' gentle mischievousness, I thought about those who want to destroy the homes of these people. Public housing has always had bad press in Melbourne. While living on them does come with challenges (I lived on the Richmond estate as a teenager), it is remarkable to witness the ability of people to create strong communities from Brutalist architecture.

My second thought was somewhat involuntary. Watching the kids walk by the Fitzroy Town Hall, where I had climbed up and down the stone steps many times as a child, I saw myself yet again, following in my older brother's footsteps. I could also see many other kids who I shared the streets with for the first ten years of my life; children whom I never saw again once our homes were demolished. Not only are my memories ghosted, but the children themselves never grew up in my consciousness. They also became ghosts.

On the morning I was caught up in the army of children, I also reached back to memories that are strictly not my own. These are the memories of my father's childhood, passed on to me through his stories. During the 1930s, 40s and beyond, many Aboriginal children ran along Napier Street and George and Little George Streets making their

Above: Tony and Wayne Birch, ca. 1960, Fitzroy, Australia, image courtesy of author.

way to the same primary school. These were the children relegated to the so-called 'opportunity grades' at George Street state school, where they were given a limited education before being spat out to become the factory fodder of industry.

The late Aboriginal activist and intellectual leader, Bruce McGuinness, lived in Fitzroy from a young age. He remains an inspiration for generations of Fitzroy Blaks. Whenever people would ask him to tell them about his Country, where he came from, Bruce would inform them that he was a product of 'Tram-track Dreaming,' the streets of Fitzroy. Aboriginal people of the inner city of Melbourne are this city. And the endless kilometres of tram-tracks that cross it, from east to west, north to south? I think of them as the conduit for storytelling, our carrier pigeons of memory. Whether you walk this city for the first or one hundredth time, you are obliged to remember that you were here, as it will always remember you.

WHAT'S LOVE GOT TO DO WITH IT

Robyn Sweaney

Topophilia—a term popularised by the geographer and writer Yi-Fu Tuan, describes the affective bond between people and place: a love of place or attachment to it. At its heart, it is a connection that encompasses the emotional, cognitive and psychological ties individuals form with their environments. This bond may manifest as a strong sense of belonging or cultural identity, or as a quiet appreciation for the particularities of a place or home.

It is a great word to describe my art practice of over twenty years—which has involved investigating the complexities of identity and place by responding to and depicting domestic Australian environments, both rural and urban. I am drawn to the uniqueness of the Australian landscape and intrigued by how homes and streetscapes function as aesthetic incarnations of belief structures. These belief structures can influence human behaviour on emotional, intellectual and spiritual levels. My house paintings focus on the everyday, modest and well-loved suburban or beachside homes, once so common they were often overlooked or even derided as lacking architectural significance. These particular houses recall the streetscapes I grew up in or passed through; their often humble home designs influenced by postwar austerity measures.

I grew up in Mt Waverley, then an outer suburb of Melbourne, in a modest, rectangular, flat-roofed house designed by migrant architects John and Helen Holgar. During the 1960s and 1970s the suburbs slowly grew around us. My father worked in advertising alongside many artists and designers. He was keen to paint and on family camping holidays brought along canvas boards and paint in the hope of finding time to be creative but raising five children left little opportunity for such creative pursuits. I still have his palette hanging in my studio. Though drawn towards studying visual arts, I was gently persuaded to pursue the arts through teaching, eventually graduating with an art teaching degree from Melbourne State College. For many years, teaching visual art in secondary schools and leading adult education classes complemented and supported my art practice.

Thirty-five years ago, I moved to Mullumbimby in northern New South Wales. The rural landscape and small country towns felt a world away from the city I had left behind. The towns reminded me of the suburbs of my youth with their verdant landscapes and humble houses. With young children of my own, I turned to ceramic vases and flowers from the garden as my subject.

Then after a decade juggling motherhood and painting, I began to change direction, sourcing subject matter from outside the home.

I had always been interested in architecture, particularly modernism and postwar buildings and how people choose to live. While riding around town one day I had an epiphany—by painting houses I could combine an expression of place with philosophical and poetic ideas. This took me outside the domestic realm of the home and the feminine associations of the still life. At that time Mullumbimby was changing with an influx of people moving to the area. I wanted to capture something of the town I knew and had grown to love.

In 2006, I had my first exhibition of paintings depicting local houses. The exhibition entitled *The House Beautiful*, was named after a book designed in the late nineteenth century by Frank Lloyd Wright with text by William Herman Winslow.[1] The book addresses the aesthetic, practical, social and spiritual concerns of creating a home. As I created this body of work, it became clear that the paintings portrayed homes, not just houses. Like a portrait painter, I aimed to capture something of the essence, character and mood of my subjects. I also strove to capture the emotional responses they instilled in me as I viewed the houses at particular times of the day.

More recently, I have been thinking about the dichotomy of 'permanent impermanence' and the philosophical problem of time and change and what it means to be 'at home.' The concept of 'home' not only conjures ideas of safety and security but also enables intimacy and individual freedom. While change is inevitable, our human need for shelter, security, safety and contentment remains constant. In this age of housing unaffordability, mortgage stress and homelessness, the idea of 'home' is being challenged. For many, home ownership is out of reach. Renting a modest house or room, or living in a tent, car, shed or caravan has become more common.

Above: Robyn Sweaney, *Summer Romance*, 2024, acrylic on polycotton.

The houses I paint are among many that capture a sense of what a home can be. Often modest in scale and built with austerity in mind, they are the homes of ordinary people who have created an intimate, unique environment for themselves.

They are based on real places but fictionalised, with elements added or removed to create the desired composition and emotional response. They may feel familiar, trigger a memory or suggest an unknown or imaginary story. They may or may not exist in this form today, which adds to their mystery. They are, unfortunately, fast disappearing from our landscape as the values and expectations of homebuyers change.

The concept of 'home' has been challenged and adapted over the years, influenced by economic shifts and other forces. In recent decades, rising wealth and growing expectations for scale and design have significantly altered the types of houses being built. As a result, the external face of our urban landscape has become radically different, especially in cities and along the coastal fringe of Australia.

The disappearing nature of these particular houses makes them all the more significant. By spending long hours carefully capturing their essence in paint, I honour them, giving each a quiet focus and value, if only for a moment.

My works are mementos of the lives that have existed—and continue to exist—behind the once familiar street facade. They are my homage to the art of the modest home built with and for love.

01 Frank Lloyd Wright, William C. Gannett and William H. Winslow. *The House Beautiful* (Auvergne Press, 1898).

Above: Robyn Sweaney, *Long Road Home*, 2021, acrylic on polycotton.

Above: Robyn Sweaney, *Love Wins*, 2021, acrylic on paper.

Above: Robyn Sweaney, *Dwell—Walking Softly*, 2019, acrylic on polycotton.

BUILDING THE ENGINE

IN CONVERSATION WITH FATOU DIEYE , POLICY AND DESIGN CONSULTANT ON ARCHITECTURE, SUPPLY CHAIN MECHANICS AND SUB-SAHARAN AFRICA'S NEXT GENERATION OF GREEN AND INCLUSIVE CITIES.

Fatou Dieye

Your system needs nourishment from both directions, a framework and then inputs. How do we build that in other contexts? In the same way I did with my T-shirt, analyse the process from concept to full dissemination. Then develop a system which considers the realities on the ground and the different inputs from the parties involved. You need the vision, skills and labour from below and then a framework from above.

- Fatou Dieye on designing systems

Fatou Dieye is a design and policy consultant previously the Managing Director of Skat Consulting's offices in Rwanda, Burundi and DR Congo, Co-ordinator of the Swiss Cooperation's construction industry transformation program for Africa's Great Lakes Region. As well as team leader for the Affordable Housing and Neighborhood Development Unit for the City of Kigali. Inflection *co-editor Alec Gutteridge sat down with Fatou to talk about care, urbanism and responsive system building.*

Your approach reflects a profound sense of care, not only for the environment, but also for the social and economic empowerment of local communities. Could you speak to the motivations behind this methodology? What influences or experiences have shaped your understanding of architecture as a vehicle for care and systematic transformation?

I obviously, personally care a lot about the continent of Africa. I was born in the West, my dad's trajectory was to leave the continent to make his way in the world and then mine is now to go back and contribute there. There has been a lot of meddling hands in Africa, a lot of decisions that were made that were not serving local interests. I see an incredible opportunity now, with discussions about the environment, with people's concern about migration coming from the African continent. To say, OK, that's fine. How can we use that to our benefit? Use this opportunity to say; give us the opportunity and you'll see what we can do.

We are seeing growth in Africa on a scale that is unprecedented. The energy we are seeing is once in a lifetime. I moved to Kigali in 2013 and the change, in terms of urban transformation, that I've seen, in the last decade, is something that could only be witnessed during this period. When I was working for the government, you would see a building on Monday and by Friday that building was gone and there would be a new road. It was mind-boggling. So that energy and that vision is, for me, thrilling, energising and incredibly humbling.

In Rwanda, the government is so clear about what they want, but the road map to get there has not been written. So, we are asked to meet the moment, to use this time and use this energy to figure out how we can care for ourselves on this continent first, for once and not have that energy extracted to care for others outside of the continent. However, by looking after our communities, our land, our environment, for our benefit, that will eventually benefit the world as well, if we're not producing huge emissions and mass migration is mitigated. So the self-care is an act of global care, but it really starts with Africa caring for itself. I think it's a beautiful moment and I'm humbled that I get to be a part of it. Some days I feel like a fake African because I was born elsewhere and I'm coming back. But I have the desire to contribute—this idea of holding hands to get the work done has been a really moving experience for me. It has helped me to see clearly, that this momentum, we must take advantage of it. We have no choice.

Your work is pragmatic, but there is this obvious interest in humans and human relationships, specifically reciprocal and mutually beneficial relationships. Do you ever think in terms of love or care? How do you relate to those concepts as a practitioner?

Okay, so absolutely, I think mutually beneficial relationships are the best way we can take care of one another. In order to encourage people and communities to be stewards of the land; to properly manage their resources, it also needs to be something that's in their best interest in the first place. In their best interest economically and their best interest socially; in terms of their community. My job is to set up those relationships so people can meet their economic needs, so they can have the room for generosity, giving, love and sharing. If you can't meet your basic needs for shelter, food and education for your children, you have no space to be giving—no matter how much you want to be or how much you value the natural resources around you and understand that they need to be managed properly.

So, all I really want to do is try to create a little breathing room for people by helping them to realise more economic possibilities so they can do that sharing, that extra community building, that otherwise seems so onerous when your resources might be limited or strained. Well, that's what we try to do, but it's all trial and error, because some things don't work, some things really don't work. These are people's lives and livelihoods and so if you don't create the right conditions, then it can really backfire on you

During our work in Kigali, we equipped these travelling brick makers. Though once they realise that they had the upper hand—because they are the only people with the skills and equipment—they can flip that rather quickly. They can start to increase prices and team up with developers and you can't be surprised by that. You need to rebalance the equation. What that means is that we haven't met their needs. So, we need to look at the design of the system we are establishing or the equation of the package that we're offering people, so that they don't feel they have to take more than is reasonable.

I think love and care is a good barometer. If someone cannot increase their level of care, then the work that we are doing is not properly calibrated. Ideally, if we get it right, then there is that extra room or space for people to do the caring—to look beyond themselves.

Were those kinds of responses unexpected? Did you have contingencies in place if people tried to manipulate the systems you were trying to develop?

That one, I should have seen that coming, but I didn't. We were trying to set up a win-win relationship between a developer with a need for materials right now and a supplier who has production facilities of their own to manage. So, we set up a short-cut. However, that relationship between that builder and those mobile teams of brick makers, our team hadn't thought out what the pitfalls of that relationship could be, or that they could band together to monopolise production in that area. But some of the relationships within the brickyards we established, were easier to predict. A brickyard owner might want to exploit workers; force them to work extra hours, separate the men from the women, give the women the more onerous lower paid task. That type of thing we foresaw, because those are traditional labour relations. So, we had ready policies and incentives that encouraged a brickyard owner to treat their staff better. That was all built in, designed in the system early on. But this particular problem was not foreseen. I can laugh about it now, but at the time you feel fury at the situation, yet this is how the private sector works.

Let's be clear that development in India, or Africa, or any place, should be driven by the people themselves and their business interests, right? So, the private sector is critical and there are going to be things you can't control. That's business. You can only hope to control ethics in business so much but you want to create the conditions where development can happen without encouraging exploitation.

Previous Page Top Left: Fatou Dieye. Sketch 1 (2025).
Previous Page Bottom Left: Fatou Dieye. Sketch 2 (2025).
Previous Page Opposite Top Right: Fatou Dieye. Sketch 3 (2025).
Previous Page Bottom Right :Fatou Dieye. Sketch 4 (2025).

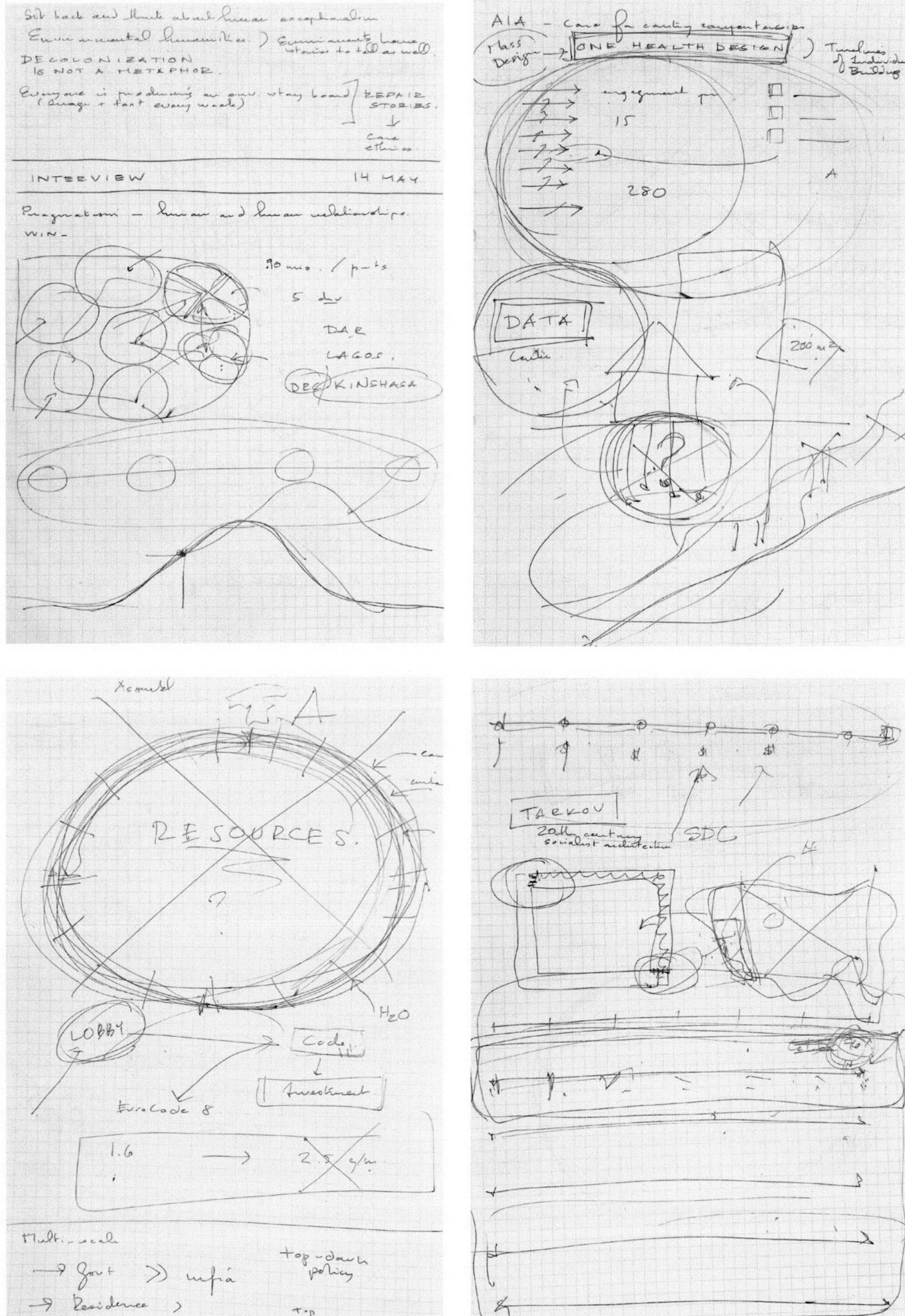
DECOLONIZATION
IS NOT A METAPHOR.
REPAIR
STORIES.
INTERVIEW
14 MAY
DAR
LAGOS.
KINSHASA
AIA
Mass
Design
ONE HEALTH DESIGN
15
280
DATA
RESOURCES.
LOBBY
Code
Eurocode 8
1.6
TARKOV
20th century
socialist architecture
SDC

I think love and care is a good barometer. [...] If we get it right, then there is that extra room or space for people to do the caring, to look beyond themselves.

What skills will architects need to develop do this kind of work? You've emphasised that a building exists within a broader system of policy frameworks and supply chains and that architects must be equipped to navigate and leverage these structures to create contextually responsive design. Why is this systems-based approach critical to our practice and in what way does it benefit local communities?

You need to know what you don't know, which is a lot. Your biggest muscle or tool is not how well you draft or how well you render—it's how resourceful you can be. So, I know what I don't know very well, but I know who to ask and I know how to ask the right questions. That is not something you are taught in school, you can start to form that type of sensitivity when studying, but that's really something you develop in the field. You must listen carefully and then build your army; those that you go to for the answers you don't have, so that you can respond to the questions that are being posed and answer appropriately.

You need to be able to identify resources and build teams. That's your biggest asset. The architecture education that is about me, me, me and my beautiful design and my building, the craft of architecture, is great. However, it is just a fraction of the process. From a technical point of view, learning how to assemble a building is something, at least in my architectural education that I didn't get enough of. It wasn't clearly defined what those connections are—between different materials, temperatures, the adjacent environment and the infrastructure or building you are planning. All those different types of connections that an architect should master, we need to do more of that in school. We need to experiment more, which might mean working at a bigger scale so that we can see the whole process with its connections and effectively manage them, as these links tend to be where problems arise.

Architectural education needs to reorient towards systems thinking. However, the education I did get, which had a heavy theoretical underpinning, is what allowed me to think like this. To understand the relationships between the conceptual, cultural, environmental. I am forever grateful that I learned to think in that way, but I need to learn how to build that way.

You wrote your thesis tracking the production process of a T-shirt in detail, supply chain management is already an established field within the fashion and garments industry. Why do you think this part of the architectural process receives less attention? Why has architecture struggled to identify this area as worthy of serious attention?

We can look to the history of the architecture profession, of who got to do it. It was seen as a conceptual and artistic enterprise. It didn't want to concern itself with the messiness of production. When architectural education started in the West, the architect wasn't the builder they were the thinker. They wanted to control the whole environment, but less so the economies which built it.

Where I live, in a low resource setting, who wants an architect? That seems like a luxury. They want engineers. The engineers do the architecture—they copy and paste plans, edit it, put it on the site, they stamp it. It's done. Nobody can afford the reflections of an architect. So, if we're going to put ourselves back in the process, why don't we become the systems thinker? If you take Frank Lloyd Wright, or Le Corbusier, who curated every detail of an environment—why can't we curate the production process in the same way? The engineer is not doing that. This is how we bring back our relevance into the system. We say, hey, listen, what we do is not esoteric or the icing on the cake, its integral. We can bring ourselves back into the debate using the skills that we already have. However, we must operate at a scale and at a technicity that cannot be denied anymore. If we start thinking as so, architecture gets the capital A. I'll never forget—I was applying for working papers to travel to Tanzania and under profession I wrote architect but when I got my visa, it said artist.

Not to devalue that, I think autographic interventions are valuable and those people are incredibly talented and imaginative at that level, we need them, they need to be a part of my community. If I am designing a system and realise there is something I don't know, or a skill I need then, I can go to the guy who's designing beautiful curtain walls the lady, who is good at gravity water systems, he can plug in here, she can plug in there. There's room for everybody. But someone has to design for that. I think we will all benefit if we do this. Now is the time, because our resources are so constrained, we're about to burn up. It is not working the way we are doing it, why not try it this way?

We will see what happens if we don't think in systems. I'm also American. With what is happening with Trump, he is going to see very quickly what happens when you cut the legs of your system. He is cutting the engine for food production. Maybe 10 people are getting very rich, but they are creating a desperate situation.

'The Rwanda New Urban Housing Agenda' reflects a multi scalar approach to design, one that acknowledges the necessity of government intervention to address systemic challenges while simultaneously empowering individual residents through innovative, flexible solutions. This model appears to strike a balance between top-down policy and bottom-up agency. How might architects working in other contexts begin to adopt and apply such a balanced and systematic approach in their own practices? What are the necessary conditions to support those architects doing that thinking?

Your system needs nourishment from both directions, a framework and then inputs. How do we build that in other contexts? In the same way I did with my T-shirt, analyse the process from concept to full dissemination. Then develop a system which considers the realities on the ground and the different inputs from the parties involved. You need the vision, skills and labour from below and then a framework from above.

I use a value chain because then it allows me to see what these inputs are. What needs to be plugged in or what the different steps are after which, you will get a housing product. However, each one these steps, each one of these value chains, is unique, it has different financial moments. A small builder in Kigali is operating using little disbursements of money for an informal house. So, the architect needs to understand that is how he operates. He says, I have a little bit of money, I add a room. I have another little bit of money, I replace my roof, I add an outside toilet, I add a renter's shack. Then, as a designer, I will then change the way that I design and deliver my house to be able to match this reality and improve and build upon what already exists. I would say to my supplier: change how you package your materials and deliver in increments.

This brings the policy, the finance from the top, in line with the realities of the local conditions. It is about the local guy. He can't build this house all at once, we need to take that into account when developing our system.

So, we design a new wall system, which can stand, if only two sides are built, because it will stay like this for a while. The builder and the architect can then work together to design what the connections at the end should be so that it can be completed when that's financially possible. This needs to be done so it fits code, or perhaps the code needs to be changed so that this is possible. As a designer, I can also do that. Your system needs to fit the top-down vision for housing coming from the government, but it also needs the flexibility to be able to respond to the local conditions. As a designer I'm bridging that gap, between the code and the reality that this builder can't build a house all at once.

Is that part of the reason you have been able to be so effective in Rwanda? As the markets and government are small and nimble enough to be responsive, as opposed to America, where these networks are so sprawling and multifaceted.

In America I wouldn't necessarily challenge established systems in this way or try to understand the whole market. So many pieces and so many gaps had to be addressed in Rwanda. It meant I had the opportunity to operate in this way. In the US, where the different value chains that make up the market are so much more firmly entrenched, as they have a longer history. It would be a lot harder, not impossible, to interrupt and rebuild those value chains.

It would be interesting in the US, because there are a lot of things broken with the construction industry and with the code. The important thing would be to recognise that the US isn't a monolith—some aspects of the code are governed nationally, but then there are also aspects that are state based, so you would look at the housing market and regulations in that state. However, California is the fourth largest economy in the world. Here, you would have to break it down even further to start to look at the value chains in that city. The markets in Rwanda are on the scale of the country, because it is so small but housing markets, could be analysed at a city level or a state level: you would assess who are the players and what are the problems.

What we did in Rwanda was as a development partner funded project, we never replaced any of the actors that were already there. Rather, we were fixing the links between two actors, seeing that a bit of information was missing, put that in the market. Then our job was to step back or create a job out of it. So, little by little, we should be invisible. These changes should exist on their own. We never funded something for somebody; we funded what didn't exist.

You need to create an economy of spare parts. In the current system, people buy their engine from overseas and their budgets are constrained. No one ever buys any spare parts. Making an economy of spare parts means you develop all the little technicians who know how to repair the engine, so when something breaks in your engine you can fix it. This way of conceptualising the project was a revolution. That is what we would do: we would create these roles for people to manage the spare parts and once that was someone's business, a part of this system, we would disappear. The skills are already there, there is incredible innovativeness amongst African youth, but we would help them develop a business model to pitch to the bank to get financed, to position themselves differently, to open up possibilities.

The Australian Institute of Architects (AIA) has implemented a new professional competency, that of Care for Country. The notion of Country comes from Aboriginal epistemologies, which define it as the sum of land, air, people, culture and myriad other practices and conditions which make up a context. In your work engaging with community and building frameworks for that engagement, what advice would you give to architects practicing in this country trying to help build these systems within Australian communities.

It is hard to do community engagement and participatory business. A lot of times, in a lot of places, it feels performative, or that you are just doing it to check the box saying, "I did a community session." I think as architects, we need to support that engagement and dialogue process. We have a responsibility there. Our value add is firstly; to understand the context and the multiplicity of voices involved in a project and secondly; if you start to design a system, you pilot it and test it out, then you give that back to the community and they transform it using their own voice. The designer says you take it and make it what you want. What makes sense to your tribe? Whether it's 15 of you or 280 different voices, you can all use the same kit of parts and just reassemble it totally differently.

So, if we can get an overall agreement about what are the pieces that should be in the kit that are authentic to all our stories, if the architect takes time to, at the beginning, set the table with the different ingredients, then they need to listen and then go and do the architecture thing of creating and making. Then give that product back and support the interpretation, the reinterpretation, of what it is that you've designed with the different communities. They will do most of the work. At the same time, you grow within each one of these communities, young people who can do that systems thinking and so the next iteration of it will come locally.

We then don't need to be there. We are there to support. We don’t want the architect sitting on the outside. We want an architect in each one of these communities who's able to do the translations necessary and continue to innovate. So, it's a tree where each branch then gives and gives, then you suddenly have multiplicity. At the beginning, however, we have to have consensus about what our parts are. So, what makes Australia, Australia? What are the things that we like that we don't like? Then we have real environmental realities—those real constraints that we need to be very clear about, real targets and a real vision. If you can get that all together then your politicians are going to have to come in and support. Your engineers are going to have to come in, your environmental scientist who's going to tell you this is going to be underwater in 10 years. We all must see the conditions clearly. And then architecture, with a capital A can get to work.

OUR INFRASTRUCTURAL LOVES AND REPRODUCTIVE LABOURS

Hélène Frichot

I would like to talk to you about our infrastructural loves, an affective endeavour which may well sound like an improbable material-semiotic conjunction. Who would think to place the pragmatics of engineered systems alongside a powerful affect like love? We did, when we collaboratively plotted our research and teaching project Infrastructural Love in the School of Architecture at KTH (Royal Institute of Technology) Stockholm, Sweden, between the years 2018-2019. Our aim was to challenge a non-critical and normative approach to architecture, conceived as: a discrete object in a field; an icon signed by an idol; and a master/apprentice dialectic.

We were initially inspired by a creative design project published in *Architecture and Feminisms: Ecologies, Economies, Technologies* by Olga Tengvall and Hannes Frykholm, one of the members of our teaching and research team (2018).[1] They had drafted a speculative experiment following a 1,289 km long abandoned rail line, Inlandsbanan, transecting Sweden. What had commenced as an industrial infrastructural project dedicated to resource extraction and colonisation extending north into the Swedish peninsula concluded with Tengvall and Frykholm's proposal for a suite of poetic-pragmatic follies; a series of encounters dedicated to relations of love. We took this prompt and decided to run a Master of Architecture design studio. A first iteration of our pedagogical dedications was named Infrastructural Love, a second, Infrastructural Care. Feminist care ethics were crucial to our pedagogical approach.[2] We learnt alongside our students. We acknowledged and respected each participant's "situated knowledges."[3] We did not disrespect our students; we listened to what they hadto say.

In *All About Love* (2000), bell hooks' love ethic implores us to "let go of our obsession with power and domination."[4] These are negative passions that still run through schools of architecture today. Instead, as she insists, we must "see our lives and our fate as intimately connected to those of everyone else on the planet."[5] Here, I would add, we must move beyond human exceptionalism in order to love and care for this damaged planet of ours. hooks writes that: "Love as a process that has been refined, alchemically altered as it moves from state to state, is that 'perfect love' that can cast out fear."[6] The alchemical capacity of love can magically transform a leaden material into gold. This is an expression of love that increases our capacity for life, rather than diminishing it. Together we can form a greater political composition and this can have a positive impact on architecture, but only if we follow a love ethic, understood as an open-ended process.

Baruch Spinoza's *Ethics* (1967) is helpful to consider when it comes to our capacity to compose a life well lived.[7]

Across the five books of his *Ethics*, Spinoza moves toward a conception of modes of life that, with effort, might achieve an intellectual love of God. When he writes of God at the beginning of the first book of *Ethics*, what must be immediately understood is not the vengeful, anthropomorphic figure concocted by priests and wizards, but Spinoza's formula, *Deus sive Natura* (God or Nature). This daring formula, which caused so much controversy at the time, defines God not as a transcendent other, but as the immanent expressiveness of Nature. Love, as well as joy, are among the most powerful and positive affects for Spinoza and both necessarily combine a body's expressive capacity with a capacity for expressing thought; that is, critical reflection.[8] The intellectual love of Deus sive Natura suggests that our work must be dedicated to planetary care, for love is shared as both a conceptual and a material practice.

Concerning Spinoza's philosophical account of love, Gilles Deleuze explains:

…the two uniting individuals lovingly form an individual which has both of them as parts, Spinoza would say. On the contrary, in the basely sensual love, the one destroys the other, the other destroys the one, what is there is a whole process of decomposition of relations.[9]

Love must construct a greater composition, rather than decomposing one part of the composition in favour of the other; such oppressive power relations are not associated with love. Furthermore, the parts or bodies in question are not only human bodies, but any kind of body. In *Spinoza: Practical Philosophy*, Deleuze expands on what we might understand by a body: "A body can be anything; it can be an animal, a body of sounds, a mind or an idea; it can be a linguistic corpus, a social body, a collectivity."[10] Such are the constellation of bodies with which architecture might conjoin to express itself, human bodies, natural bodies, conceptual bodies, infrastructural bodies.

Below: *Infrastructural Love*, 2022, eds. Hélène Frichot, Adrià Carbonell, Hannes Frykholm, Sepideh Karami.

In her *Notes Toward a Performative Theory of Assembly* (2015), Judith Butler insists that infrastructural and environmental conditions cannot be disassociated from a capacity to live and act in a world.[11] Our infrastructural systems support the places in which we gather and supply the basic utilities of life. We must argue for our rights of access to infrastructural goods, too many of which have been privatised with the global hold of an avaricious neoliberal capitalism. An infrastructural body here pertains to the spaces in which we assemble, the coming together of bodies (both human and non-human) in those spaces and the conceptual bodies that are circulated as we argue for our shared commonwealth, our matters of concern and our matters of care.[12]

What we insist upon in our book *Infrastructural Love* (2022) is that "Infrastructural love as an affective orientation encourages a radical engagement with the world, putting the architect in close proximity with that which requires support and exposing the architect to the risks of such encounters."[13] We were of course careful to elaborate the ambivalent qualities of infrastructure in its entanglement with architecture, suggesting that, on the one hand, infrastructure supports *colonising* projects (such as the rail-line that transports resources and imperialist intent), but on the other hand, as a material-semiotic matrix it can enable *decolonising* potentials. Infrastructure, we argued "requires constant care and maintenance to ward off failure, and yet the moments of failure are when the act of love as radical work makes space and opens opportunities for gathering and working together."[14] Here we place an emphasis on care ethics and relate this to a fundamental expression of reproductive labour. Acknowledging that homework maintenance undertaken by women and minorities has been historically undervalued, we included in our research and teaching deliberations the importance of engaging intersectionally across gender, sexed difference, class, racially marked bodies and differently abled bodies. Critical Studies in Architecture was well known for such critical and creative approaches.[15]

Infrastructual love pertains to institutions too. I was employed as a civil servant for eight years in a Swedish institution of higher education. In that context, students are not designated as units of value because education is free. A work/life balance is respected, especially as many students are of a mature age with young families and other commitments. Data is protected under strict EU laws; a student would never be asked to sign away such privacy protections. A professor would never dream of setting a deadline on the weekend and not even on a Monday, as this would assume work had to be undertaken on the weekend—inappropriate! Women in leadership are valued, not vilified. As in any institution there are disagreements, differences of opinion and position. In Critical Studies in Architecture, a research and teaching division I led between 2014-2019, we fostered a wild adventure in ideas, queer orientations, feminist design power tools, dialogical openness and participatory actions that were not disingenuous but embedded with local community. We sought to make a difference. This was the milieu out of which our infrastructural loves and reproductive labours emerged.

When education forgets its core responsibilities, a love of learning and undertaking this work collectively and collaboratively, it becomes an educational-industrial complex. Australia prides itself on what is currently its fourth largest export product: education (recently demoted from third position in the aftermath of COVID19 and governmental policy changes). Following coal, iron ore and natural gas, it is telling that education is figured here in a list of non-renewable and environmentally destructive resources. This order of things begs the question of the modes of extraction at work when it comes to education denominated as an export industry. There is no love lost in these sorry relations and these sad passions. What we need is love and relations of care that push back against the anti-intellectualism and fear of critical thinking that has taken hold like a wily weed. All we need is love…

01 Olga Tengvall and Hannes Frykholm, “Infrastructural Love.” Hélène Frichot, Catharina Gabrielsson, Helen Runting eds. *Architecture and Feminisms: Ecologies, Economies, Technologies* (Routledge, 2018), 212-217.

02 Hélène Frichot, Adrià Carbonell, Hannes Frykholm, Sepideh Karami, “Our Infrastructural Loves: Architectural Pedagogies of Care and Support.” *Journal of Architectural Education*, vol. 76, Issue 2 (2022): 52-69. https://doi.org/10.1080/10464883.2022.2097509.

03 Donna Haraway, “Situated Knowledges: The Science Question in Feminism and the Privilege of Partial Perspective.” *Feminist Studies* 14, no. 3 (1988): 575-599. https://doi.org/10.2307/3178066.

04 bell hooks, *All About Love: New Visions* (Harper Collons Publishers, 2000), 87.

05 Ibid, 88.

06 Ibid, 93.

07 Baruch Spinoza, *Spinoza's Ethics and on the Correction of the Understanding* (Everyman's Library, 1967).

08 See: Moira Gatens and Genevieve Lloyd, Collective Imaginings: Spinoza, Past and Present (Routledge, 1999) and Hélène Frichot, “On Finding Oneself Spinozist: Refuge, Beatitude and the Any-Space-Whatever,” in *Gilles Deleuze: Image and Text*, eds. Charles J. Stivale, Eugene W. Holland,Daniel W. Smith (Continuum Press, 2009), 247-263.

09 Gilles Deleuze, Lecture Transcripts on Spinoza's Concept of Affect, Cours Vincennes, 24/01/1978. http://www.webdeleuze.com/php/sommaire.html.

10 Gilles Deleuze, *Spinoza: Practical Philosophy* (City Lights Books, 1988), 127.

11 Judith Butler, *Notes toward a Performative Theory of Assembly* (Harvard University Press, 2014), 64.

12 For a discussion of 'matters of concern' and 'matters of care' see Bruno Latour, “Why Has Critique Run Out of Steam,” *Critical Enquiry* 30 (Winter 2004): 225-248 https://doi.org/10.1086/421123; Maria Puig de la Bellacasa, “'Nothing Comes without Its World': Thinking with Care,” *Sociological Review* 60, no. 2, (2012): 197–216, https://doi.org/10.1111/j.1467-954X.2012.02070.x; Maria Puig de la Bellacasa, *Matters Of Care: Speculative Ethics in More Than Human Worlds* (University of Minnesota Press, 2017).

13 Adrià Carbonell, Hannes Frykholm, Sepideh Karami “Infrastructural Love: Caring for Our Architectural Support Systems, ” in *Infrastructural Love: Caring for Our Architectural Support Systems*, eds, Hélène Frichot, Adrià Carbonell, Hannes Frykholm, Sepideh Karami, (Birkhäuser, 2022), 12

14 Ibid, 23.

15 See Hélène Frichot, *How to Make Yourself a Feminist Design Power Tool* (AADR, 2016) and Meike Schalk, Ramia Mazé, Thérèse Kristiansson, Maryam Fanni eds, *Feminist Futures of Spatial Practice* (AADR, 2017).

MACHINES FOR ATTUNEMENT

MINOR ARCHITECTURES IN THE SHADOW OF LOVE

Felix Garner-Davis & Nina Nervegna

Mirrorwork

Fishermans Bend may be Naarm/Melbourne's densest palimpsest; or pentimento, if we trace that word to its root, *paenitere*—to regret, or repent. Either way, this place is troubled. Its atmospheres, spaces, surfaces, and objects are more than an archive, and more than a ghosted overlay. They materialise anthropocentric weather.

Here, we settlers find ourselves refracted: warped, crystalline. We are steel, asphalt, silt, runoff. We are constructed parkland, traffic-island flora, warehousing, embankment—and the contaminated lap of river against it. We are Coode's shipping canal, slashed through swamp. Northerlies spin freight dust into cul-de-sacs and derelict lots. Gulls circle cranes. Puddles gather rainbow films, fed by leaking sumps.

The land is visibly and invisibly overcoded by industry, policy, and speculation. It is at once an erasure field, an industrial precinct, a development horizon, and an unsettled ecosystem. It is a crucible, too—"for a spectral mode of love," in which attention to entanglement becomes both architectural method and ethical task.[1]

The funnel found us.

Storm
saturated the subsoil—

filled our spiderpit
with liquefied street
and stratum.

Our helical flight—
up, where we corroded,
gazing into char:
ultraviolet
corneal rubying.

Guests quartered a cow,
silent.

We felt sick.

The world is an undersized grater.

Provisional Mesh

This piece is part of a project we commenced in 2023. It occurs here, in Fishermans Bend, because its territory is unstable; and because instability—economic, aesthetic, ecological, epistemological, ontological, neurological—frames our architectural praxis and its substructure, including the poetry and artmaking that seeded it.

We started designing for nonhumans after digesting books on metaphysics and animal ethics. These explorations—like many others—continue to infuse our work, and we view the public realm as its most philosophically coherent path. There, in Naarm/Melbourne's small-practice architectural ecology, civic opportunities are doubly destabilised. They are often driven by low-budget, design-insensitive municipal procurement processes, and are consistently pressured by the design-and-construct sector.

These commissions—shade structures, pavilions, public-toilet upgrades, community-centre refurbishments—are not glamorous, but they are the cartilage of the civic skeleton, and they present unassuming chances for design excellence. They are also structurally provisional. Briefs may be indecipherable or inaccurate, or may seek unpaid return-briefing before a contract is awarded. Tenders may be lost on price by a few hundred dollars, or may be issued without any certainty of work being undertaken. Projects may vanish between budget cycles. Bureaucracy and maintenance issues may complicate the durability of completed buildings and renovations. Nonetheless, we now theorise this provisionality not as an obstacle, but—in parallel with Helene Frichot's teaching on object trajectories at the Melbourne School of Design—as a material.[2] Here, provisionality is not a cage, but an instructive, asymmetric armature. It is a substrate, prompting us to sculpt layers of entangled inquiry. We believe it can support a mode of architectural behaving, being, and knowing—an entwined ethic, ontology, and epistemology—that nourishes compositional and intellectual expression by reconfiguring compromise.

This mode is a design stance grounded in process, with implications beyond plan and section. In contrast to segmented, solutionist, masculinist philosophies that pursue clarity through compartmentalisation, we might term it "ethico-onto-epistemological," after Karen Barad.[3] It is pliable, adaptable, and it opens space for what we call, in accord with Jill Stoner, "minor architectures"[4]—small, prosthetic design gestures that deterritorialise dominant logics from within, dense with ethical and affective charge.[5]

a far mound,
we witness a tree
accelerate through age,
sprout-gnarl branches
in curlicues.

The sense
is of poison—
a syringe slow-pierced
into root tissue
scuffed visible by dig.

Globes ascend,
droning.

Subfrequency—
a cavern
of molten sound;
pharynx of antennae

prickling,
umbilical depression
above.

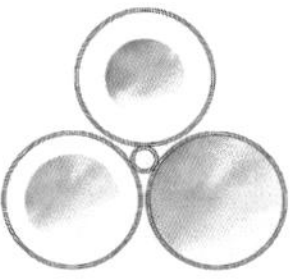

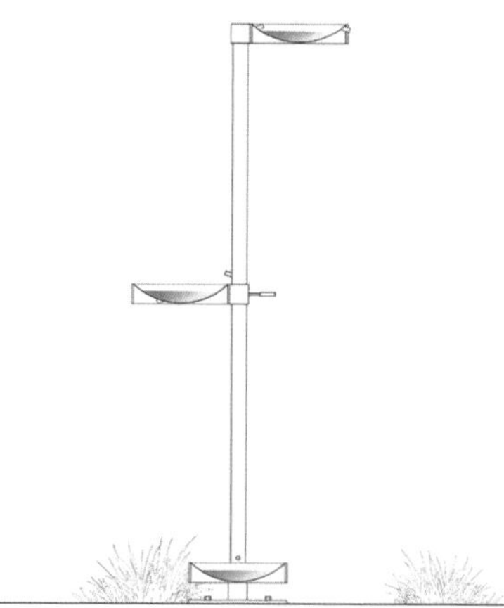

Little Door, Vast Room

Minor architectures are self-consciously peripheral. Against the field's ongoing preoccupation with mastery (even along many of its covertly hegemonic fringes), they are inversions of normativity. The minor eye scans. The minor ear parses sales talk. The minor hand fumbles. Eventually, it draws, nurturing little structures that unfurl questions of dynamic, transdisciplinary resonance. They enable not just partial but substantial agitation of hierarchical assumptions, even reverberating ontologically—by disturbing the primacy of human existence—in ways that many tendencies in other aesthetic disciplines still avoid, like poetry that privileges the "lyric I."

Asphalt cartograph,
holed soil—

some hypercube,
undulating

abalone
hydrofoil, rising
iridescent
through shrugged crumbs
of clod.

Your warm hand
folded in mine.

A root hums;
crystallising tendrils
of hyphae crawl
into filigree,

wrapping a trunk.

Calyx,
wavering.

Minor architectures can be conventional, speculative, or both, and resist the temptation to scale up as a measure of significance. They sidestep the logics of prestige that dominate architectural culture and development economies. Imagine a bat roost bolted to a pier girder; a fungal inoculator in a median-strip stump; a rain-sensing sound device strung from a streetlamp. Their success is measured not in foot traffic, press, or client curiosity, but in a quieter register: the return of nightjars to a nesting chamber; the first bloom of mycelium in compacted soil; the thrum of a gutter in a downpour; the phytofiltration of nitrogen from a slow-dripping tank.

These gestures are both conjectural and real—devices of fabulation as well as function. They reflect an architectural epistemology and ethic that emerges from dreaming and worlding, but also from procedural realities: in our case, from the unsteady mechanics of tendering, the limits of municipal budgets, the occasional flash of a sensitive project officer willing to trial something odd.

Among these petals and roots, minor praxis is the rhizome. It is the day-to-day work of helping to keep a small practice solvent while making room for such gestures. This practice could be formal or informal: a billable process of service delivery, or a recursive commitment to built-environment contemplation and knowledge production. For us, depending on luck, it may be both—or just the latter.

Regardless, by principally concerning itself with "making room," minor praxis is inseparable from its exhalations—from minor architectures themselves. It enables them, and illuminates the ideas they adjoin, including their own core operation of making room for more-than-human possibilities—through doors so small they risk invisibility or ridicule. This act of allocation, of making room, is the key. Praxis becomes practice becomes thinking becomes praxis. As we sketch birdsong, we hear it intensify. Tendrils grow, bifurcate, interlace. One informs the other. Each keeps the other supple.

Spectral Love as Eco-Gothic Method

If provisionality is our material, spectral love is our method: an ethic of care that neither denies harm nor seeks purification, but works through residues and impurities. This is love's shadow—imperfect, unresolved, and frequently in tension with the forces it reflects and hopes to reorient. It resists reinscribing commercial culture's veneer of exceptionalism and solutionism, instead advocating a practice of attention that carries grief, obsession, and monstrosity within its affective range. Spectral love aligns with Sara Ahmed's argument that emotions are not private states but social orientations: they reveal unacknowledged relations and press our bodies into them, often uneasily.[6]

The "eco-gothic," a subfield of the environmental humanities, is where this love finds its architectural idiom.[7] Gothic conventions chart love as embodied, compulsive, and uncertain, while the eco-gothic extends these intensities—via ecocriticism—into contaminated, extractive landscapes like Fishermans Bend.[8] Space and material are pollinated with feeling, which operates as a critical mechanism. It ventriloquises and registers the anxieties of environmental crisis, as Elizabeth Parker and Harriet Stilley note while describing the journal Gothic Nature.

Among these emotive textures, repair is never restorative; it cannot reinstate a past condition. Instead, it makes futures differently liveable. Karen Barad's "agential cuts,"[9] and Donna Haraway's notion of "response-ability," articulate this stance: commitments to stay with the trouble while experimenting with ethical intervention, rather than trying to resolve it prematurely.[10]

In Fishermans Bend, the trouble is palpable. Petrochemical yards abut public paths; stormwater outfalls darken the river; batching plants shed dust. In this zone, prosthetic interventions take on a double charge: they acknowledge toxicity, then fold another use into it. A bee hotel grafted near an exhaust stack does not cleanse the plume, but reframes it as vertical terrain where pollination and petrochemical residue cohabit. A salt wick drawing brine from water—like the crystallised car lodged beneath the surface of Westgate Park's Pink Lake—traces mineral scars, registering climate encroachment rather than masking it. A fungal windharp transforming decay into soundscape renders entropy audible. A set of modules under the Salmon Street bridge utilise its empty undercroft for artist residencies. Above them, sprouting gutters arc, trimming the carriageways. Their steel fins glint. Leaves absorb chromium. Stems separate oil from rainfall.

These prostheses are not solutions, but invitations to inhabit dissonance—and to acknowledge that we already do. Spectral love, expressed in an eco-gothic mode, argues that architecture works most powerfully not by dispelling unease, but by holding it: attending to sorrow, toxicity and persistence.

Silent, paralytic grid.
Subzone: yolking.

We trace an aperture
together.

Showed me the vein
first spoiled,
before the rest followed;

time is marked
by your tentative sips.

The russet dusk,
darkening
dropped peach;

bladed slant
of a fog-sluiced shiplight—

wavelets shiver.

A quiet octopoid breach.

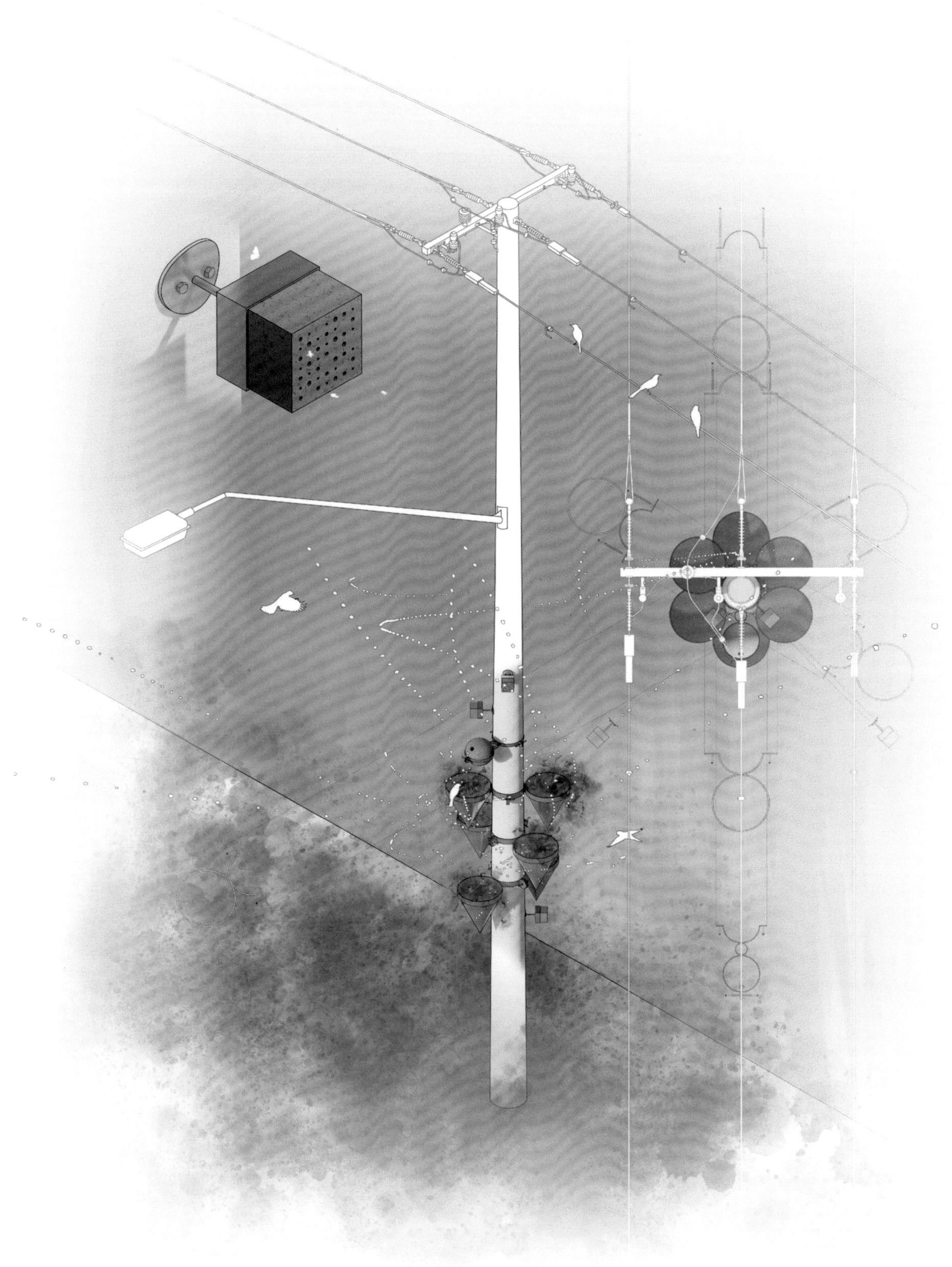

Procedural Realism

Love becomes praxis when speculative ethics meet the procedural grind. A tender for playground renewal might specify "pergola to match existing." We suggest drawing a planted canopy, sown for pollinators. In most cases, it would be value-managed out. In some, it could survive.

Such manoeuvres adapt to turbulence. A prosthesis might be designed as modular, installable in stages as budgets allow. It might be instrumentalised: pitched rhetorically, in alignment with published policy priorities. While the territory is arid, every crack reveals a hinge where council strategy and more-than-human ethics could pivot together.

We are testing this approach in practice through a bolt-together nursery for Westgate Park, commissioned by Bili Nursery, Westgate Biodiversity, and the City of Melbourne. These organisations carry the spectres of two grassroots we knew as children: the St Kilda Indigenous Nursery Cooperative and the Port Phillip Ecocentre.[11]

Sited under the bridge, on a windswept sliver beside Boeing's aerostructure factories, the project extends minor-architectural principles—modularity, civic prosthesis, habitat provision—into an operational setting, under timeline and multi-stakeholder constraints. It balances ecological and cultural ambition with cost, maintenance, and council process. Speculative design becomes procedural realism: a site-specific prototype for attunement.

This mode of practice looks unremarkable from the outside: narrow allocations, incremental improvements, adjustments buried in tender packages, fragments of habitat smuggled into routine civic works. However, these are the interstices through which minor architectures grow. Against spectacle, procedural realism advances by persistence and repetition, by learning the idioms of civic procurement and bending them toward other ends.

It is also a practice of patience. Most gestures do not endure: they are stripped out for cost, postponed across budget cycles, or erased by shifting priorities. To work this way is to live with repeated disappointment—and to continue. That persistence is itself a form of care: a willingness to remain with civic rhythms that are slow, frustrating, yet fertile.

In this sense, procedural realism is not the opposite of speculation but its companion. It grounds dreams in the temporality of bureaucracy, where even slight dissonances can resonate. It is a form of attunement: not to an idealised design future, but to the everyday moments through which small public works, and the lives they touch, come into being.

We watch the river
circulate a spiral
of nitrogen—

our lilypad
buoyed by its crenations
in the current.

The orb—
teal opalescence,
hovering moss.

A susurrus.

Radial linework:
spoked periwinkle core,
glistening
in flicker.

We draw closer
to the infrasound
shrouding its black splinters—
a transparent sphere,

distorting the willow
behind.

Machines for Attunement in the Capitalocene

Our prosthetic interventions are machines. They connect, collect, divert, host, and shield. They are also devised to attune human and non-human bodies to shared conditions. Attunement is a sensory recalibration: a reorientation of how one inhabits space. These machines are resonators—tuning forks. They vibrate, establish resonance, invite response.

A tripartite fountain offers water to dogs, birds and people. A network of planters on power poles transmits pollen-legged butterflies, reconnecting the Royal Botanic Gardens with Westgate Park. A freeway sign becomes a wildlife crossing. A nestbox shelters wagtails. A myco-bench in a riverside park, built from mycelium-bound panels, asks its sitter to share time with decay's quiet metabolism. A spider gallery on a bridge truss frames webs against the sky, recasting arachnid presence as tracery. These interventions do not moralise or preach. They stage atmospheres that linger after the encounter, carrying a minor charge of dislocation and recognition.

Their field is the Capitalocene: our geohistorical condition.[12] Futures are patterned by extractive logics, and Mark Fisher's concept of "capitalist realism," naming a mutual epistemological limit, insists that no alternatives exist: that it is easier to imagine the end of the world than the end of capitalism.[13] In this context, minor architectures resist through disproportionate offerings. They do not aim to solve systemic crises, but to interrupt inevitability. An owl hollow will not "fix" Fishermans Bend. However, it creates a slender cut in the development-as-destiny narrative.

As Karen Barad identifies, each "agential cut," or intervention, enacts a material-discursive incision in the fabric of possibility.[14] In practice, these cuts are often too normative to register: a thick, sectional line through a drawing; a price or scope chop to keep a tender alive in a downturn. Even then, they are also conceptual fissures: disruptions that make new relations thinkable.

Machines for attunement carry dual force: they recalibrate perception, and slice into inevitability. Their value lies less in permanence, and more in the affective and ontological shifts they instigate—provisional, but real.

Our swingset creaks,
falls
into oxide ash.

A pulse.

Fingers of aquifer
emerge
through peat,
sputtering,
gyrate upward—

accelerant plaits,
each a geyser
in unison twist.

A dome of silk.

Love, Complicity and Staying with the Trouble
Love in the shadow is necessarily complicit. To work in the city is to participate in its ecologies of harm. We draw salaries from councils that invest in highways. We specify materials from destructive supply chains. We inhabit infrastructures of settler-colonial extraction. The question is not how to remain or become pure, but how to work with impurity—how to turn complicity toward repair, without pretending that harm has been erased.

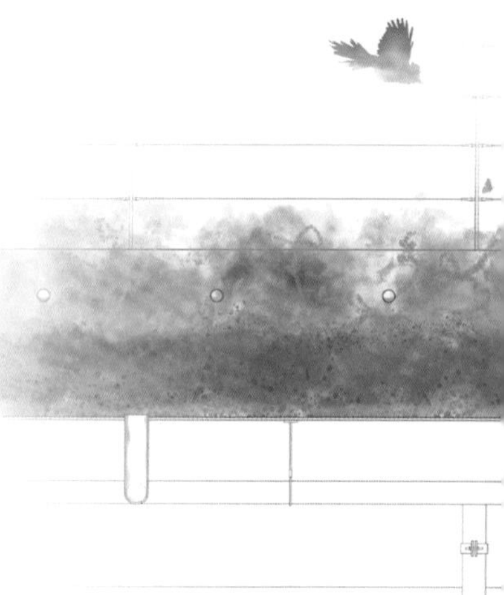

This is where the eco-gothic intimately converges with practice. Beauty, horror, care and decay are inseparable; they surface together in architectural gestures. A bat roost attached to a warehouse may, within five years, be demolished for apartments. Yet for a time it shelters a colony, seeds conversations, and reframes a skyline. A propped branch for boobooks may rot, happily clawed. A salt-encrusted wick may vanish with waterbody management, but in the meantime it renders climate fragility tangible. These acts are provisional, but they resonate, neither denying nor disguising impermanence.

To stay with such gestures is to accept architecture's limits while refusing its abdication. It is a discipline of complicity, but also possibility. As Donna Haraway teaches us, trouble is ongoing, irreducible, and not to be engineered away.[15] Accordingly, minor architectures are chords struck in the composition of the city—intervals that recalibrate attention rather than monuments that endure. They show that even small, civic-oriented practices, working under budgetary precarity and bureaucratic inertia, can create openings where other ways of living-with become perceptible.

From a drone scan, these openings may be invisible. Yet on the ground—in a bat's wing, a salt-shard bloom, the hum of a mildewed windharp—they register as something else: a spectral love made tangible, ghosted by alterity. If we suppress anthropocentrism and quietism, along with our predilection for solution and salvation, we may locate a practice that dwells with complicity, acknowledges harm, and keeps crafting nonetheless.

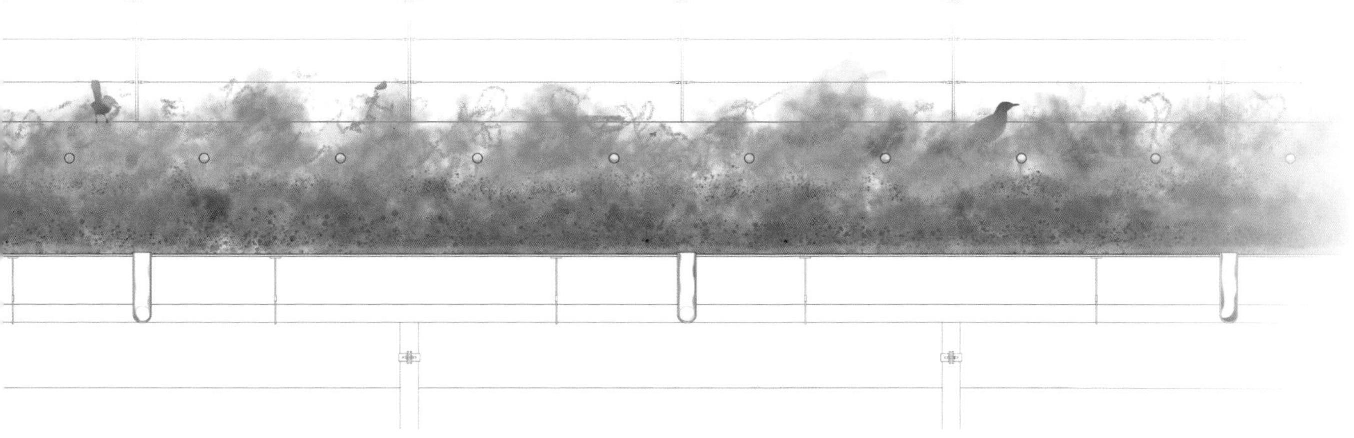

One—
your fallen tear,
venturing

into my—two—
fallen hands,
cupped.

Three;

four eyes—
one fixed,
two filling.

The beep.

Fingers pressing.

Oculus,
ghosted
by a dusting sunbeam.

Five—

the dilation, percussion
of iris:
dissipating

the eye.

01 María del Pilar Blanco and Esther Peeren, eds., *The Spectralities Reader: Ghosts and Haunting in Contemporary Cultural Theory* (New York: Bloomsbury Academic, 2013), 8.
02 Hélène Frichot, "ABPL90421: Design – Philosophy – Architecture," https://handbook.unimelb.edu.au/2025/subjects/abpl90421.
03 Karen Barad, *Meeting the Universe Halfway: Quantum Physics and the Entanglement of Matter and Meaning* (Durham: Duke University Press, 2007), 89–90.
04 Jill Stoner, *Toward A Minor Architecture* (Cambridge: MIT Press, 2012), 22–23.
05 Gilles Deleuze and Félix Guattari, *Kafka: Toward a Minor Literature*, trans. Dana Polan (Minneapolis: University of Minnesota Press, 1986), xxiii.
06 Sara Ahmed, *The Cultural Politics of Emotion* (Edinburgh: Edinburgh University Press, 2004), 10–11.
07 Elizabeth Parker and Harriet Stilley, "About the Journal," *Gothic Nature: New Directions in Ecohorror and the EcoGothic*, https://gothicnaturejournal.com/about-the-journal.
08 Andrew Smith and William Hughes, eds., *EcoGothic* (Manchester: Manchester University Press, 2016), 5; Elizabeth Parker, *The Forest and the EcoGothic: The Deep Dark Woods in the Popular Imagination* (Cham: Palgrave Macmillan, 2020), 3–5.
09 Barad, *Meeting the Universe Halfway*, 139–141.
10 Donna Haraway, *Staying with the Trouble: Making Kin in the Chthulucene* (Durham: Duke University Press, 2016), 34.
11 Bili Nursery and Westgate Biodiversity, "SKINC's Story," https://westgatebiodiversity.org.au/our-histories/skinc.
12 Haraway, *Staying with the Trouble*, 47–48.
13 This idea is referenced in Mark Fisher, *Capitalist Realism: Is There No Alternative?* It has also been discussed by Fredric Jameson and Slavoj Žižek.
14 Barad, *Meeting the Universe Halfway*, 139–141.
15 Haraway, *Staying with the Trouble*, 3–4.

LOVE SHACK

Thomas Essex-Plath

What is there left for architecture to love? For the last couple of millennia, it has flirted endlessly with other disciplines. The list of half-hearted betrothals (to geometry, history, philosophy, music, medicine, jurisprudence, astronomy) that Vitruvius included in *De Architectura*[1] in the first century BC pales in comparison to the number of disciplines that have appeared in the citation lists of an architectural profession now firmly ensconced within the twenty-first century academy. Typically, these relationships have amounted to little more than wolf-whistling out the window of a passing car. Love, on the other hand, is a unique kind of commitment. Not simply a fleeting passion, or even an enduring tie sustained by adoration or fascination, but a holding-fast to something. Following Graham Harman (following Dante), it is a devotion not merely to the appearances or relations of an object but to its entirety, to its substantiality and thus its unrevealed inner depths.[2]

An object much worthier of architecture's love is also much closer: the everyday, the ordinary, all that familiarity brings near to us but also makes transparent, inconspicuous and unnoticed. Not this or that thing that might be called everyday or ordinary, but the aspect of everydayness itself.

Architects make occasional avowals of affection for the everyday. Stock phrases on websites and in monographs declare a concern for "the everyday" or "everyday life," and contemporary trends in architectural imagery have sanctified but deflated the everyday into a laconic, picturesque scenography. But these little love letters to everydayness, with no one daring to follow through on their doting gestures, do more harm than good. Not only is there no true engagement with the everyday, but they also pervert it, fetishise it, reduce it to a pin-up on their bedroom wall. This distorted, aestheticising enthusiasm for the ordinary may bring a tendency to "patronise, colonise, and extract from" the everyday, but this precipitates from a misplaced attachment to an 'everyday' rather than to 'everydayness' itself.[3]

To really fall for everydayness is to consciously cultivate the underexplored potentialities of building that are unveiled by ordinary and familiar buildings and the events they are entangled with: the capacity to seem anonymous or unauthored; to genuinely go unnoticed, by either peers or publics; to rejected rarified, fashionable tropes in favour of common, generic and ordinary features and ways of ordering them; to embrace the repeated, the copied and reiterated project, rather than grasp vainly at originality; to laud loose compositions of parts and see the folly in 'pure' wholes and attempts for authorial control; to demonstrate the messy, concrete realities of construction and shirk the reductionism of abstraction; to articulate the poetic potentials of ambiguity, make mannerist plays with conventionality, turn attention to revealed depth and encounter the uncanny; to dissolve boundaries between 'architecture' and 'mere building,' and the social distinctions and class divisions that are naturalised through them; to understand and (re) interpret the mundane processes and practices that these buildings are a constitutive part of, which create and sustain the patterns of societies with their routine, cyclical temporality.

This particular object of love, though it might be a source of delight, or contentment, or revelation, or fascination, is a terrible, indeed terrifying thing. It is terrifying in its inescapable pervasiveness, its insidious influence, its thinness, its levelling down, its homogeneity, its featurelessness, its sheer banality. Most unsettlingly, when we encounter the contingency and groundlessness of the everyday we fall head-first into confronting the awful, sublime reality of our own finitude. This is not some pure, flawless, divine object of love, but a troubling, Janus-faced reality. A levelling down that forever draws towards an inauthentic and 'fallen' life, yet the only ground for both intelligibility and 'authenticity.'[4] It is the site for the reproduction and focus of alienation, yet the recoverable residue of the 'real' and integrated life.[5] It is saturated with subjugating 'strategies,' yet the space for resisting 'tactics.'[6] So, it can only be with the steadfast commitment found in love that architecture can hope to sustain a relationship with everydayness.

A love of everydayness is terrifying for architecture for the same reason why love is always frightening: we might lose ourselves in it. This is the great, looming peril of the everyday for architecture. Vast swathes of ordinary, anonymous buildings have their origin in something outside the world of architecture. In their magnitude, they are a threat; they seem to suggest (indeed, may even be evidence for the fact) that the architect is unnecessary. More fundamentally, to love everydayness is terrifying because extraordinariness is too close to the core of architecture's self-definition; to embrace the ordinary would seem to negate those distinctions of exceptionality ("A bicycle shed is a building; Lincoln cathedral is a piece of architecture") on which the discipline is founded.[7]

But this threat to architecture's identity, this reason why it might flee from it, is the same reason why it ought to pursue it. To fall in love is, ultimately, a transformative experience; to do it well is to become better. This is why architecture must cultivate a love for everydayness. For too long (maybe always), architecture has defined itself through inventively diverse means of articulating its exceptionality. A cavalcade of different forms of obtrusive idiosyncrasy, uniqueness and distinction, along with our compulsions to produce them and our distorted self-image as artistic creatives, is the result. These, in turn, have

Above: Heinrich Tessenow, Row Houses in Hellerau, 1910, Germany, photograph by Thomas Essex-Plath.

been the leash handed to those who have gladly taken advantage of us, whether as a vehicle for conspicuous consumption and the display of social distinction, or for the production of icons that legitimate powerful institutions and their enterprises, or to provide superficial market differentiation and brand identity for profit-driven development and the financialisation of basic needs. To fall for everydayness is to open up the possibility of being released from these compulsions and all the toxic relationships that they have landed us in. Giving up the myths of heroic, individualistic, artistic authorship that fuel these compulsions is easier when the everydayness of architectural labour itself is encountered with lucidity: its mundanity, but its contingency, its messiness, its collectivity, its prosaic materiality, its heterogeneity, its dependencies, its anonymity, its conventionality.[8]

However, to fall for everydayness would not be to submit blindly and in entirety to it, nor merely reproduce ordinary built fabric, or take it as a given, as necessary, as universal, or as unchangeable. An architecture of everydayness does not seek to simply reproduce or reinforce extant patterns of everyday life. Rather, this sensibility approaches any particular everyday with careful criticality, attentive to what ought to be reconfigured rather than reproduced. It is only through articulating everydayness, bringing the background of familiarity to the fore, that architecture can establish the basis for critically engaging with it. To really come to terms with everydayness is to discover latent potentialities in the contemporary condition and to allow or encourage these to unfold; interrogating and testing the extents of the agency architecture might have. The everyday, too, is transformed through this love.

01 Vitruvius, *The Ten Books on Architecture*, trans. Morris Hicky Morgan (Dover Publications Inc., 1960), 5-6.

02 Graham Harman, *Dante's Broken Hammer* (Repeater Books, 2016).

03 Beatriz Colomina and Mark Wigley, "Foreword" in *Everyday Matters: Contemporary Approaches to Architecture*, ed. Vanessa Grossman and Ciro Miguel (Ruby Press, 2022), 7.

04 Martin Heidegger, *Being and Time*, trans. John Macquarrie and Edward Robinson (Harper and Row, 1962).

05 Henri Lefebvre, *Critique of Everyday Life*, trans. John Moore and Gregory Elliot (Verso, 2014).

06 Michel de Certeau, *The Practice of Everyday Life*, trans. Steven Rendall (University of California Press, 1984).

07 Nikolaus Pevsner, *An Outline of European Architecture*, 7th ed. (Penguin Books, 1968).

08 In this effort, the sociology and anthropology of architectural practice is especially valuable: see, for example, Judith R. Blau, *Architects and Firms: A Sociological Perspective on Architectural Practice* (MIT Press, 1984); Dana Cuff, *Architecture: The Story of Practice* (MIT Press, 1992); Robert Gutman, *Architectural Practice: A Critical View* (Princeton Architectural Press, 1988); Magali Sarfatti Larson, *Behind the Postmodern Façade: Architectural Change in Late Twentieth-Century America* (University of California Press, 1993); Albena Yaneva, *The Making of a Building: A Pragmatist Approach to Architecture* (Peter Lang, 2009); and Thomas Yarrow, *Architects: Portraits of a Practice* (Cornell University Press, 2019).

Left: Sergison Bates Architects, Islington End-of-Terrace Housing, 1999-2002, United Kingdom, photograph by Thomas Essex-Plath.

Right: Richard Stampton, House on Phillip Island, date unknown, Australia, photograph by Thomas Essex-Plath.

LEARNING TO LOVE:

A NEW VISION OF EDUCATION AND PRACTICE

William Ward

A lament I often hear from architecture students is that, fundamentally, architecture is "designing houses for rich people." Of course, this observation does not capture the range of sectors and clients that make up professional practice, but there is more than some truth to it. Architecture's client base is typically made up of organisations, governments and private individuals with some form of capital exceeding that of the average citizen. The steady erosion of public investment means that firms can rarely afford to take on more spiritually enriching projects and the cost of architectural services—always a tough sell—is increasingly hard to justify.

The discipline of architecture has always presented its contributions as a service to the public good. This belies an expectation that the public will, in some way or another, express some affection for our gifts. For much of its history, architecture has positioned its "aesthetic gifts" as its chief contribution to the public good and therefore the measure of its value.[1] Given that the public's idea of 'good' architecture is now often the exact inverse of the profession's, this assumption is somewhat unnerving.[2] This unequal relationship does not seem especially beneficial to either party. In her book *All About Love: New Visions*, the American author bells hooks suggests that Western cultures typically think of love as a commodity that can be given and taken away at a moment's notice.[3] This definition of love provides a very tenuous foundation for individual and communal relationships. Instead, she thinks of love as an ongoing process between parties requiring trust, openness and compromise. Her reframing transforms love from an object that one can possess to a process whose meaning derives from its constant negotiation. hooks' alternative definition of love seems more conducive to a healthy relationship between architecture and the public it serves.

Given the many crises the world is facing, the profession must reckon with its historical dependence on the wealthy and powerful. Here too, hooks' vision of love seems far more useful than its alternative, but reforming a discipline that has developed across two millennia is not straightforward. An effort to re-define architecture first requires a reading of its history.

A History of the Profession's Self-image

In Stephen Parcell's telling, the profession's origins in ancient Greece were quotidian compared to its eventual elevation to one of the Beaux-arts of the late seventeenth century.[4] 'Architecture,' a noun referring to a set of practices constituting a discipline, did not exist as such. For the ancient Greeks, an *architekton* (chief builder) coordinated other *tekton* (craftspeople) in the construction of public buildings. This role necessitated a working knowledge of natural materials that were the basis for other *techne* (crafts) and an awareness of how ancestral building traditions might contribute to the *polis*.[5] Crucially, ancient Greek society drew no distinction between the status of architect and craftsperson.

The classical Greeks and Romans viewed building as a vulgar art, distinct from the seven liberal arts, whose contributions were better aligned with the advancement of the public good.[6] Vitruvius sought a definition of architecture in line with Plato's epistemological model, where buildings, as with other products of human labour, could be judged against a set of 'first principles' typical of 'ideal' natural forms.[7] This left little use for the ancient Greek *technē*, whose knowledge constituted ancestral craft traditions that had emerged without guidance and would continue to develop in the same manner. Vitruvius' new definition codified architecture as a higher pursuit with its own practical and theoretical knowledge and, consequently, elevated the architect above the builder.[8] In the fifteenth century, Leon Battista Alberti framed architecture as a liberal art and the architect as an intellectual whose knowledge and practices were scientific, further entrenching the discipline's distance from mere craftsmanship.[9] In the late seventeenth century, architecture assumed Beaux-arts status which Parcell argues continues to define the discipline's epistemology today.[10] The admittance of architecture to the Beaux-arts positioned it awkwardly alongside painting, sculpture, poetry and music. Aesthetics became the shared rubric against which the five fine arts could be judged, necessitating a further reduction to architecture's contributions to the common good.

While most schools of Modernism had explicitly political aims, histories of the period emphasise their innovations as aesthetic in nature. Modernism's grand ambitions to transform society were widely seen as megalomaniacal and homogenising, driving Charles Jencks to declare its death and with it the proposition that architecture could directly catalyse social change.[11] Accordingly, the Postmodernists retreated to the world of semiotics and pure representation to issue critiques of society and the Deconstructivists and Post-structuralists rejected the idea of architecture as a site for resistance entirely.

Despite its political foundations, Postmodern architecture became synonymous with the aesthetic excess and commodification of the Reagan and Thatcher era.[12] The new avant-garde of the 1980s and 1990s, composed of figures like Greg Lynn, Zaha Hadid and Rem Koolhaas, displaced political theories with formal metaphors that drew from network theory, rhizomes and complex systems. Douglas Spencer sees architecture's post-political and post-critical turn as "the spatial complement of contemporary processes of neoliberalization."[13] Koolhaas, not uncritically, would describe architecture's role "as the decisive and fundamental articulation of a society" as defunct, superseded by a position of ideological pliability in deference to the whims of the free market.[14]

In this narrative, one can see the discipline's transformation from a vocation defined by communal bonds to a rarefied, intellectual profession detached from labour and valued primarily for its aesthetic novelty. The outcome of the post-political turn that began in the 1980s was a commodification of architectural aesthetics in service of the neoliberal economic project. Notwithstanding this history, the past decade has seen a renewed interest in political action within architectural theory and practice, often centred on concerns for climate and sustainability. However, the definition and scope assumed by the profession under Neoliberalism make it difficult to pursue this new direction in any meaningful way.

Love in Crisis

By many metrics, the profession of architecture is in crisis. In a recent report on the health of the architectural services industry, the Architects Registration Board of Victoria (ARBV) paints a grim picture of a hyper-competitive sector threatened by large, vertically integrated construction firms, the absorption of its skillset by other professions and automation.[15] The remuneration for architects is lower than allied professions in the construction sector.[16] The average scores of architectural professionals for the Personal Wellbeing Index sit substantially lower than the Australian average.[17] A survey of architecture students in the same year similarly observed an average level of wellbeing "much lower than Australian population norms."[18] At the risk of sounding glib, there is clearly a shortfall of love within the discipline.

Declarations of crisis from within architecture are a regular recurrence and the discipline's low pay and deleterious effects on the wellbeing of its members are well known. The causes of each are complex and difficult to quantify, but the persistence of these problems amidst worsening economic conditions is enough reason to wonder if a change is in order. The new generation of professionals may already be tired of waiting: a recent European study found that 38% of architectural graduates had entered careers other than architecture.[19]
Peggy Deamer posits that the discipline's low pay and chronic dissatisfaction are partly an outcome of its attachment to a definition of its value framed in terms of creativity and artistry.[20] Architects are encultured to believe that they, as creative professionals, do not 'work' in the same way as the other members of the 'service sector.' Historically, artistic and creative work has not been viewed as labour, despite constituting both cultural and literal capital. To Marx, "in so far as he enriches the publisher [...] the writer is a wage laborer for the capitalist."[21] Deamer links the discipline's view of its work to the way it is compensated. If the value of a building derives from its status as a work of art, then logically an architect's fee should be computed as a percentage of its total construction cost.

If one were to frame this schism as a simple public relations problem, the Trump administration has kindly prepared a curriculum of architects and styles whose aesthetic qualities might (at last!) "make architecture beautiful again."[22] Less reproachable authors have made similar cases for a return to classical standards from the opposite of the political spectrum.[23] The architectural critic Elizabeth Farrelly, perhaps unaware of the last few centuries of the profession's history, has recently argued that architecture should re-commit itself to the pursuit of beauty to solve its value crisis.[24] As tempting as it may sound, doubling down on aesthetics will not save architecture. This demands a far more radical project to reform the profession's identity and the nature of its value.

Emma Williamson, the government architect of Western Australia, articulates a position that encapsulates both the profession's misplaced priorities and its most promising directions. Responding to a question about how architects might "broadcast the value of architecture to a wider audience," Williamson posits that the discipline and broader society's "fixation on the consumption of imagery" impedes a much-needed reckoning with the profession's value. "To shift the focus from the object and towards its impact, "architects might first "centre [their] dialogue on the profound human and social impacts of design." For Williamson, this dialogue should involve "not just the architects who sit inside the (well-designed) tent, but anyone—and ideally everyone—who can advocate for the benefit of good design."[25] If our goal is a discipline whose contribution to the common good derives from the act of working with, not on behalf of, the public, architecture must view itself as a collaborative effort embedded in a broader social, political and cultural context.

Love and Labour

So far, I have made the case that the discipline of architecture has fashioned for itself, over the course of its 2,000-year plus history, an understanding that its value lies in the pursuit of universals. This has never been an entirely accurate description of architectural work, but the gap between the discipline's self-image and practice has grown even wider in the past two decades.
In a 2014 article for *ArchitectureAU*, Paolo Tombesi makes an argument not unlike Williamson's. He argues that we should expect modern professionals, including architects, to respect the "collective trust" that is implied by their status. This trust "carries [an] obligation to act on behalf of the community and in support of the common good."[26] Instead, Tombesi sees the real work of contemporary design as a complex, non-linear process with substantial cooperation between actors.[27] However, the strict hierarchy imposed by profit-driven development impedes genuine collaboration. The atomisation of design labour apportions responsibilities and expertise across several professions, organised into what Deamer calls a "vertical, knowledge-based hierarchy" akin to the Fordist production line.[29] The resulting intra-professional friction and resentment is an intended outcome, leading to the pursuit of efficiency over quality.

Tombesi suggests a new organisational model of practice which emphasises the "design of the project," rather than the "design of the building"—a non-hierarchical, collective structure where collaborators assume equal responsibility (and risk)—replacing the normative 'production line' model . Nishat Awan, Tatjana Schenider and Jeremy Till extend this vision beyond the construction sector. In their view, "spatial production," the fundamental work of architects, is already performed by a range of "spatial actors," including "politicians," "artists," "users" and "builders."[30] Case studies collected in recent texts such as *Architecture and Social Change* (2025), *Architects After Architecture: Alternative Pathways for Practice* (2020), *The Organiser's Guide to Architecture* (2024) and editorials such as this issue of *Inflection* demonstrate how both models might work in practice. Designers, architects and academics are increasingly working in ways that invite stakeholders normally excluded from the development process into the fold.[31]

This image of professional practice today resembles hooks' new vision of 'love' far more than the one its history offers. Architects and designers can produce social benefits when their practice transcends the borders of conventional development. If the parameters governing design are constraining, we are better off, as Keller Easterling suggests, "reformulating the equation."[32] Still, these are only isolated examples. Redefining the practice of architecture and its place in the construction sector is a transdisciplinary and intergenerational project. Given the immense pressures on architectural firms, we cannot expect practitioners to enact systemic reforms from within. A more plausible site for a speculative project is architectural education, which is less bound up in pragmatics but nonetheless constrained by its historical development.

Learning to Love

How might architectural education foster a more mutualistic, equitable design practice? The intuitive move is to model the complexity of modern design work in studios. Similarly, seeding opportunities for interdisciplinary exchange throughout the curriculum seems plausible given architectural programs and allied professions tend to share a faculty. But while simulating the 'real world' might better prepare graduates for the workplace, it does not substantially alter the borders of practice. Remaking the profession's self-image demands a curriculum with a capacity to critique the discipline and its political, cultural and economic context.

At present, architectural education invites students to engage with sociopolitical issues in individual studios, rarely as part of a structured curriculum. Accreditation leaves little room for architecture programs to challenge the mechanisms of professional practice, especially at the graduate level. The dominant view of architectural history, affirmed by students, practitioners and Performance Criteria (PC) 25 of the National Standard of Competency for Architects (NSCA), is to provide design inspiration.[33] Architectural history teaches a Euro-centric 'canon' that privileges aesthetic ingenuity over context; minority and marginalised voices are woefully under-represented.

Architectural education's organisation and pedagogy have remained relatively stable over the last century. Prior to architecture's institutionalisation, an apprenticeship system was the most common model for teaching technical skills.[34] The architectural curriculum at Academie des Beaux-Arts represents one of the first attempts to bring the apprenticeship model into the academy and remains the most influential. Students, under the supervision of a master architect, worked together on a series of design competitions in the *atelier* (studio). Students were expected to work together in the *atelier* for long stretches, with the expectation that the personal and professional bonds they formed would enculturate them into the practice of architecture.[35] While the full-scale *atelier* model is unfeasible in tertiary institutions, its pedagogical methods and signature culture persist in the design studio. Despite significant changes to tertiary institutions and the profession, architectural education relies on an outdated, under-theorised model structured around the studio.

In Australia, design studios form on average 40% of the combined undergraduate and graduate degrees.[36] Despite comprising such a large percentage of the degree, studio teaching is not grounded in an explicit pedagogical model or theory.[37] Critics highlight a range of problems: instructions and criteria are unclear or shift unexpectedly; the presence of a 'hidden curriculum' of cultural and social norms; and, in particularly extreme terms, the reliance on fear to motivate learning.[38] Paradoxically, the studio served as the basis for Donald Sch n's 1983 study *The Reflective Practitioner*, which has significantly influenced the pedagogies of many disciplines beyond architecture.[39] Taken together with the importance that students, practitioners and educators place on the studio, we can assume it is a reasonably effective method for delivering an architectural education. However, given its many problems and lack of theoretical background, we are also justified in asking more of it.

Design work is rarely a solo pursuit in practice, but the lone genius myth is pervasive in studio, the historical canon and representations of architects in popular media. As is the case for most pedagogies in higher education, the studio model emphasises individual performance through graded assessment. The goal of this assessment, often implicitly, is to measure students' creativity, a quality that is under-theorised and notoriously hard to measure.[40] Wilson and Zamberlan suggest that an understanding of creativity as a collective phenomenon is more appropriate for design in the twenty-first century.[41]

Instead, the studio could become a site of 'critical inquiry,' where students and educators develop, apply and extend their knowledge in a setting that more closely resembles the real work of design and the context it operates within.[42] As well as bringing the standard curriculum in line with contemporary design practices, architectural education could become a testing ground for design techniques, stakeholder relationships and professional roles that are presently difficult or implausible under the prevailing development model. Kirsten Day and her co-authors suggest that stakeholder mapping, role playing and, where possible, co-design with community members can form an expanded view of architectural work that privileges the process, not the artefact.[43]

What constitutes 'knowledge' in a design studio can include other areas of the curriculum that are often disconnected. Day et al. suggest that 'de-professionalising' professional practice subjects by detaching them from accreditation criteria would create space for a more critical, contextual approach to topics such as project management, business skills and legal responsibilities.[44] If learning related to the profession was dispersed across the curriculum rather than concentrated in a single subject, students and educators could critique existing arrangements, understand them as part of a historical trajectory towards profit-driven development and explore alternatives. While my goal is not to aid the march toward vocationalisation, a more holistic approach to professional practice might also quell practitioners' persistent demands for a more 'job-ready' workforce.[45]

In the same way, architectural history could adopt a more critical and context-laden position towards its existing canon. A truly critical approach to the Modern movement, for example, might approach the canon with greater awareness of racialised and fascistic views held by many of its proponents.[46] Architectural history might find itself more valued by students if it were to focus less on the aesthetic merits of canonical works by white Europeans and more on social, cultural and political forces that shaped their practice. Martina Tanga and her co-authors propose an interdisciplinary approach to art and architectural history, where the "symbolic and affective" mode of the former informs a reading of spatial manifestation of the latter and vice-versa.[47] Additionally, more emphasis on the profession's responsibilities and its position in broader society could inform critical inquiry elsewhere in the curriculum.

Lastly, architecture's admission to the academy has meant a greater emphasis on design research.[48] The introduction of a two-year graduate degree also extends this expectation to students. Many of the principles above are being developed through design research within the academy. More-than-human and interspecies design envisions owls, mosses and trees as co-designers, which often necessitates collaboration with ecologists, biologists and Traditional Owners.[49] There are valuable lessons for educators, practitioners and students in research that tests the limits of who (and what) can participate in design.

If this is all to work in a university context, design studios need to move away from expecting individual students to produce a 'complete' project in fourteen weeks. Instead, assessment could emphasise investigation of multiple scenarios and their concomitant stakeholders and processes. A greater focus on group-work is necessary, but its use in design assessment remains controversial. Learning to work together is a skill like any other, but students are rarely supported to develop it.[50] Educators need to communicate the value of group work and its centrality to design and design assessments that reward collaboration, not problematise it.

Just as we cannot expect practitioners to overhaul the profession, educators cannot design a new curriculum for a version of architecture that does not yet exist. A key tenet of critical pedagogy is that students should have agency over their learning.[51] This takes on even more importance in design, where the freedom to develop one's own creative practice is integral to learning. Educators, practitioners and most of all students, should chart a map of the new territory of architectural practice together. There is a growing body of pedagogical research calling for a new process-driven, community-oriented model of architectural education—the will to reform education and practice is palpable. Given the impetus for change, why is education clinging to its old models?

The Unbearable Weight of Accreditation

A recurring theme in this discussion of architectural education is the fraught relationship between professional bodies, tertiary institutions and practitioners. In Australia, the laws that protect the title 'architect' and regulate tertiary qualifications necessitate a way of accrediting Master of Architecture programs. The Architects Accreditation Council of Australia (AACA) ensures that graduates of accredited institutions meet the Performance Criteria set out in the National Standard of Competency for Architects. An institution may offer degrees without accreditation, but because they cannot provide a pathway to registration as an architect, they are essentially worthless. In effect, the AACA has immense sway over the curricula of graduate-level architectural programs through the auditing process. Accreditation must be understood in the context of the financialisation in the tertiary sector that began in the 1980s and has accelerated since the early 2000s.[52] Growing class sizes, shrinking facilities and precarious employment for staff all complicate efforts to move towards a process-driven model of architectural education. An institutional culture of managerialism, bureaucratic oversight and aversion to risk has led to the prioritisation of performance criteria in assessment at the expense of pedagogical innovation.

Professional and regulatory bodies are not blind to the priorities of their current and incoming clientele. The Australian Institute of Architects (AIA) and Architects Accreditation Council of Australia (AACA) have recently taken positions on housing affordability, reconciliation with Aboriginal and Torres Strait Islander peoples and the climate crisis.[53] These are undoubtedly positive moves, but they occur in the context of a construction sector that is hostile to change. Using 'performance criteria' to advance these goals places the burden on architects to resist developer actions that would violate their professional responsibilities—it is hard to imagine this going well, given the power imbalance.

More broadly, the profession is overdue for a reckoning with its protected status and the registration regime needed to enforce it. The ARBV's 2022 report on the health of the sector claims that navigating the present crisis will require innovative approaches and new models of practice.[54] The irony here is that the regulations the Board enforces preclude the possibility of such innovation. Kirsten Orr notes a "chorus of voices within the profession" that suggests a misalignment between the definition of practice expressed in the NSCA and reality.[55] In a climate of growing risks, the registration is starting to resemble a sleight-of-hand trick that saddles the worst-paid with the most legal burden. Deamer suggests de-professionalisation might democratise the discipline and halt the creep of contractualisation.[56]

Towards Another Architecture

Architecture, in the terms it has traditionally defined itself, has no hope of combatting the defining problems of the twenty-first century. De-carbonising the built environment, democratising the housing market and serving marginalised stakeholders are "wicked problems" that implicate multiple disciplines, sectors and stakeholders.[57]

Confronting them will require a reckoning with the discipline's relationship to the public, which is fraying under immense economic pressure and threatening to unravel completely. The dire conditions facing the sector are partly a cause of its attachment to an antiquated, hermetic definition of itself. Architecture's "aesthetic gifts" are at best a tenuous foundation for a loving relationship with the public it serves, who are increasingly the most privileged members of society. There are growing calls from within the discipline to find new ways to convey its value; the most promising candidates emphasise design as a practice that is embedded in and practiced in partnership with communities.

Professional practice cannot address these concerns within the constraints imposed by the profit-driven construction sector and architectural education's fealty to outdated, theory-less models limits the scope of innovation by the next generation of architects. If architecture is to restore its social mission, it must start by reforming its system of education. Educators and researchers are already working to ground design education in pedagogical models, but they need the support of the profession. The limits accreditation imposes on architectural education are stifling progress and are difficult for institutions to resist. A re-assessment of the need for professionalisation is overdue.

Learning to Love Ourselves

This article was borne out of my experiences as an architectural educator. Today's students are frustrated by a curriculum that presents a model of practice with no hope of addressing housing affordability, climate action and social justice. Utopian studio briefs that ignore architecture's context tend to raise more questions than answers. Architectural education is marching steadily towards professionalisation, led by the demands of accreditation bodies and employer interest groups. Its outdated pedagogy encultures students into an anachronistic model of individual practice that they have little interest in.

Today's aspiring architects face a job market with an oversupply of graduates. If they are lucky enough to find a job, their remuneration will be substantially lower than their peers with 'lower' qualifications requiring fewer years of study. The narrow definition of practice set by accreditation is evidently on the verge of collapse. Sending students into this economic maelstrom borders on predatory. The curriculum is built around a set of skills that are specific to an outmoded model of practice, limiting the degree's transferability and placing the burden of training on struggling firms. The high rate of graduates leaving for other professions suggests that students are taking matters into their own hands. University students are remarkably critical people. They are well aware of the zero-sum game they are walking into. I am confident that they hold the solutions to the discipline's problems, because they share them with me every day. Their vision of architectural practice is one attuned to the needs and desires of the many, not the few; a practice whose value is earned by listening, deliberating and co-operating with stakeholders that architecture normally excludes. The pathway to an architectural practice that serves the common good is already being outlined in a growing body of design and pedagogical research.

I believe that this new vision of architecture has a good chance of restoring the public's trust in the profession. If we're lucky, they might even love us back.

01 Peggy Deamer, "Deprofessionalisation," in *Architecture's Afterlife: The Multisector Impact of an Architecture Degree*, ed. Harriet Harriss (Routledge, 2024), 187.

02 William Fawcett et al., "Reconciling the Architectural Preferences of Architects and the Public: "The Ordered Preference Model," *Environment and Behavior* 40, no. 5 (2008): 599–618, https://doi.org/10.1177/0013916507304695.

03 bell hooks, *All About Love: New Visions* (William Morrow, 2018).

04 Stephen Parcell, *Four Historical Definitions of Architecture* (McGill-Queen's University Press, 2012), 250.

05 Ibid., 23–24.

06 Ibid., 249.

07 Ibid., 38.

08 Ibid., 39.

09 Andrea Čeko et al., "What Is Architecture? A Contested History of the Discipline and Its Embeded Meanings," in *Architecture's Afterlife: The Multisector Impact of an Architecture Degree*, ed. Harriet Harriss (Routledge, 2024), 25.

10 Parcell, *Four Historical Definitions of Architecture*, 250.

11 Charles Jencks, *The Language of Post-Modern Architecture*, 5th ed. (Rizzoli, 1987).

12 Mary McLeod, "Architecture and Politics in the Reagan Era: From Postmodernism to Deconstructivism," *Assemblage*, no. 8 (1989): 38, https://doi.org/10.2307/3171013.

13 Douglas Spencer, *The Architecture of Neoliberalism: How Contemporary Architecture Became an Instrument of Control and Compliance* (Bloomsbury Academic, 2017), 1.

14 Philipp Oehmke and Tobias Rapp, "We're Building Assembly-Line Cities and Buildings," *Der Spiegel,* December 12, 2011, https://archive.is/iTxbn.

15 Architects Registration Board of Victoria (ARBV), *Systemic Risks in the Australian Architecture Sector* (ARBV, 2022), 91, https://tinyurl.com/yc4ywsxs.

16 c.f. Hays, "Hays Salary Guide FY24/25," *Hays*, 2024, https://tinyurl.com/bdfyfpja; Association of Consulting Architects Australia (ACA), "2023 Salary Survey Findings," ACA, 2023, https://aca.org.au/2023-salary-survey-findings/.

17 Tracey Shea et al., *The Wellbeing of Architects 2023 Practitioner Survey,* Primary Report (Monash University, 2023), 25, https://thewellbeingofarchitects.org.au/publications/the-wellbeing-of-architects-2023-practitioner-survey-primary-report.

18 Tracey Shea et al., *The Wellbeing of Architects 2023 Student Survey,* Primary Report (Monash University, 2023), 6, https://thewellbeingofarchitects.org.au/publications/the-wellbeing-of-architects-2023-student-survey-primary-report.

19 Harriet Harriss, ed., *Architecture's Afterlife: The Multisector Impact of an Architecture Degree* (Routledge, 2024), xi.

20 Peggy Deamer, "Work," in *The Architect as Worker: Immaterial Labor, the Creative Class and the Politics of Design*, ed. Peggy Deamer (Bloomsbury Academic, 2015), 61–62, https://doi.org/10.5040/9781474244046.ch-005.

21 Karl Marx, "Productivity of Capital/Productive and Unproductive Labor," in *Theories of Surplus Value,* pt. 1 (Lawrence and Wishart, 1969), 401; quoted in Deamer, "Work," 64.

22 *Making Federal Architecture Beautiful Again, Executive Orders* (2025), https://www.whitehouse.gov/presidential-actions/2025/08/making-federal-architecture-beautiful-again/.

23 Adrian Rennix and Nathan J. Robinson, "Why You Hate Contemporary Architecture," *Current Affairs*, October 31, 2017, https://www.currentaffairs.org/news/2017/10/why-you-hate-contemporary-architecture.

24 Elizabeth Farrelly, "Are We Dollarising Architecture to Death?," *ArchitectureAU*, June 23, 2025, https://architectureau.com/articles/are-we-dollarising-architecture-to-death/.

25 Emma Williamson, "Emma Williamson on How to Broadcast the Value of Architecture to a Wider Audience," *ArchitectureAU*, January 29, 2025, https://architectureau.com/articles/emma-williamson-on-how-to-broadcast-the-value-of-architecture-to-a-wider-audience/.

26 Ibid.

27 Paolo Tombesi, "The Responsibility of Designing," Discussion, *ArchitectureAU*, 2014, https://architectureau.com/articles/the-responsibility-of-designing/.

28 Paolo Tombesi, "On The Cultural Separation of Design Labour," in *Building (in) the Future: Recasting Labor in Architecture*, ed. Peggy Deamer and Phillip Bernstein (Princeton Architectural Press, 2010), 126.

29 Peggy Deamer, "Detail Deliberations," in *Building (in) the Future: Recasting Labor in Architecture*, ed. Peggy Deamer and Phillip Bernstein (Princeton Architectural Press, 2010), 83.

30 Tombesi, "On The Cultural Separation of Design Labour," 131–133.

31 Nishat Awan et al., *Spatial Agency: Other Ways of Doing Architecture* (Routledge, 2011), 11–12, https://doi.org/10.4324/9781315881249.

32 Brian Holland, ed., *Architecture and Social Change: Shaping an Impactful Practice* (Routledge, 2025); Harriet Harriss et al., eds., *Architects After Architecture: Alternative Pathways for Practice*, 1st ed. (Routledge, 2020), https://doi.org/10.4324/9781003007753; Kirsten Day et al., *The Organiser's Guide to Architecture Education*, 1st ed. (Routledge, 2024), https://doi.org/10.4324/9781003411284.

33 Keller Easterling, *Medium Design: Knowing How to Work on the World* (Verso, 2021).

34 Architects Accreditation Council of Australia (AACA), *National Standard of Competency for Architects 2021*, version 1.0, Architects Accreditation Council of Australia, May 2023, 6, https://aaca.org.au/wp-content/uploads/2021-NSCA-Explanatory-Notes.pdf.

35 Michael J. Ostwald and Anthony Williams, *Understanding Architectural Education in Australia* (Australian Learning and Teaching Council, 2008), 1:11.

36 Ibid., 1:19.

37 Alex Maroya et al., *Architectural Education and the Profession in Australia and New Zealand* (Architects Accreditation Council of Australia (AACA), 2019), 46, https://www.aaca.org.au/wp-content/uploads/Architectural-Education-and-The-Profession-in-Australia-and-New-Zealand.pdf.

38 Barbara De La Harpe and J. Fiona Peterson, "Through the Learning and Teaching Looking Glass: What Do Academics in Art, Design and Architecture Publish About Most?," *Art, Design & Communication in Higher Education* 7, no. 3 (2009): 135–54, https://doi.org/10.1386/adch.7.3.135_1.

39 Jan Silberberger, "What Can Possibly Go Wrong? Three Examples of Recurrent Deficiencies in the Teaching of Architectural Design," *International Journal of Art & Design Education*, 2022, 244, https://doi.org/10.1111/jade.12409; Philip Crowther, "Understanding the Signature Pedagogy of the Design Studio and the Opportunities for Its Technological Enhancement," *Journal of Learning Design* 6, no. 3 (2013): 20, https://doi.org/10.5204/jld.v6i3.155; Colin M. Gray, "Critical Pedagogy and the Pluriversal Design Studio," *Design Research Society*, June 25, 2022, 6, https://doi.org/10.21606/drs.2022.238.

40 Donald A. Schön, *The Reflective Practitioner*, 1st ed. (Routledge, 1992), https://doi.org/10.4324/9781315237473.

41 Stephanie Elizabeth Wilson and Lisa Zamberlan, "Design Pedagogy for an Unknown Future: A View from the Expanding Field of Design Scholarship and Professional Practice," *International Journal of Art & Design Education* 36, no. 1 (2017): 108, https://doi.org/10.1111/jade.12076.

42 Ibid., 112–113.

43 Ashraf M. A. Salama, *Spatial Design Education: New Directions for Pedagogy in Architecture and Beyond* (Ashgate, 2015), 174.

44 Day et al., *The Organiser's Guide to Architecture Education*, 40–41.

45 Ibid., 87.

46 For example, see survey results in: Maroya et al., *Architectural Education and the Profession in Australia and New Zealand*, 83.

47 Irene Cheng et al., eds., Race and Modern Architecture: *A Critical History from the Enlightenment to the Present* (University of Pittsburgh Press, 2020).

48 Martina Tanga et al., "Counterplanning from the Classroom," *Journal of the Society of Architectural Historians* 76, no. 3 (2017): 278, https://doi.org/10.1525/jsah.2017.76.3.277.

49 Caroline Voet et al., *The Hybrid Practitioner: Building, Teaching, Researching Architecture* (Leuven University Press, 2022), 9.

50 Stanislav Roudavski, "Interspecies Design," in *Cambridge Companion to Literature and the Anthropocene*, ed. John Parham (Cambridge University Press, 2021).

51 Ostwald and Williams, *Understanding Architectural Education in Australia*, 1:136.

52 Joe L. Kincheloe, *Critical Pedagogy Primer*, Peter Lang Primer (Peter Lang, 2004).

53 Maroya et al., *Architectural Education and the Profession in Australia and New Zealand,* 24.

54 Architects Accreditation Council of Australia (AACA), *National Standard of Competency for Architects 2021.*

55 Architects Registration Board of Victoria (ARBV), *Systemic Risks in the Australian Architecture Sector*, 83.

56 Kirsten Orr, "Institutionalising National Standards," *Architects Accreditation Council of Australia*, 2015, 15, https://aaca.org.au/wp-content/uploads/Institutionalising-national-standards_Assoiate-Professor-kirsten-orr_2015.pdf.

57 Deamer, "Deprofessionalisation."

58 Horst W. J. Rittel and Melvin M. Webber, "Dilemmas in a General Theory of Planning," *Policy Sciences,* no. 4 (1973).

THE ARCHITECTURE OF RELATIONALITY

IN THINGS WILL BE DIFFERENT AND THE MERRI NORTHCOTE PUBLIC HOUSING RENEWAL PROJECT

Celeste de Clario Davis

Above: Graffiti at Walker Street Estate, 2019, photograph by Celeste de Clario Davis.

On the corner of High Street and Walker Street in Northcote sits one of Victoria's latest public housing renewals, Merri Northcote. The redevelopment consists of six modern buildings nestled into the banks of the Merri Creek on Wurundjeri Country. Unlike the brash Postmodern apartments that pervade the city, Merri Northcote avoids ostentatious complexity. Its design is uniform and pared back, with certain in-vogue features indicating the stylistic imperatives of a socially conscious, design-oriented homeowner. These details include exposed concrete walls, terrazzo tiles, earthy tones, recycled materials and a "relaxed connection to the natural environment," all of which amount to the renewal's architecturally chic presence—an aesthetic synonymous with the building's architects, Six Degrees.[1] Nevertheless, Merri Northcote—formerly known as the Walker Street Public Housing Estate—and despite its progressive facade, is symbolic of Victoria's state-led erasure of public housing.

In 2019, the then-impending 'renewal' of the Walker Street Estate as a dispersed assortment of privately owned properties (with only a perfunctory addition of community housing) became the catalyst for *Things Will Be Different* (2024), a feature-length documentary directed by Lucie McMahon and shot/produced by myself.[2] The film chronicles the forced relocation of two neighbours at the Estate when their homes are demolished under the Public Housing Renewal Program (PHRP). It explores the impact of losing one's home, the important role that public housing plays in our communities and the relationships that secure housing can cultivate. Informed by a collaborative, processual and care-centred methodology, *Things Will Be Different* invokes an alternative framework to consider how Walker Street Estate's redevelopment as Merri Northcote could have been shaped: through a mode of 'renewal' that centred the relational needs of community over profit.

The political context of the Estate's redevelopment and the film itself is the Labor government's 2017 proposal to renew 11 public housing estates within inner-city Naarm/ Melbourne under the PHRP. The program has since been rebranded as Victoria's Big Build Program and expanded to demolish all public housing estates in the city by 2051. The PHRP was introduced with the purported aim of ameliorating public housing through a large-scale renewal project that would ultimately result in more dwellings. Contrary to these claims, however, there have been several research and policy critiques outlining the detrimental implications of the proposal. In *Understanding the assumptions and impacts of the Victorian Public Housing Renewal Program*, co-authored by Dr David Kelly and Professor Libby Porter from RMIT's Centre for Urban Research, they highlight that the PHRP will result in the mass transfer of public land to a consortium of private developers and housing organisations, a decrease in dwelling capacity despite a marginal increase in dwellings and negative long-term impacts on residents and communities who live in public housing.[3]

The origins of *Things Will Be Different* can be traced back to the Save Public Housing Collective (SPHC)—a grassroots public housing advocacy group formed in response to the PHRP. In 2017, I joined the collective and was later introduced to Lucie through David and Libby, who encouraged a collaboration as we both had lived experience in public housing and respective backgrounds in lens-based media. Lucie and I initially set out to film the architecture of the Walker Street Estate, the residence of Will—my ex-stepdad, good friend and fellow public housing activist—for archival purposes. After shooting, we would spend hours talking with Will on his balcony. We discussed topics like property, the history of Walker Street, Sydney's bygone mod scene and the importance of generously interpreting a person's behaviour. These conversations shifted the project's direction, as Will expressed a strong interest in being recorded and in contributing his experience to public housing discourse. The dynamic that emerged between us all during this time forecasted the collaborative and enduring relationships that would go on to shape the film.

Lucie situates this filmmaking approach within what Bill Nichols terms a 'participatory mode', in which relationality is central to the filmmaking process.[4] This methodology inverts a teleological focus on the work's outcome, instead prioritising its process. In this sense, *Things Will Be Different* functions not only as a record of Will and his neighbours' experiences of being displaced, but also as a feedback loop that recursively reflects the relational dynamics at play in the documentary. Throughout the film, these exchanges manifest in both discernible and subtle ways. A pertinent example of this is a walking tour of the Estate conducted by Will, which he asked us to film for his own personal archive. For this walking tour, Will convened key figures involved in the redevelopment program—including developers, architects and representatives from the State Government—to explain how residents interacted with the Estate, in the hope that this insight would be incorporated into the redevelopment. This footage later made its way

Above: Lucie McMahon, Still of Will at the Walker Street Estate from *Things Will Be Different*, 2024.

into the film as its opening scene. In other instances, Lucie or I appear within frame when in conversation with Will. Here, self-reflexivity is an inescapable part of the ontological and relational dimensions within. This footage later made its way into the film as its opening scene. In other instances, Lucie or I appear within frame when in conversation with Will. Here, self-reflexivity is an inescapable part of the ontological and relational dimensions within the making of *Things Will Be Different*; that is, the embedded relationships between filmmakers and participants.

Similarly, the aesthetic of the documentary is indicative of the collective conditions it was made under. This is notable in the film's lo-fi patina and sometimes erratic cinematography, which reflects the resourceful modes of its production, utilising a borrowed, outdated video camera and drawing on my (at the time modest) cinematographic experience. Likewise, collaborations between friends and SPHC members who assisted with research and post-production contributed to an aesthetic that is symptomatic of circumstance rather than design. It is through these collective and relational occurrences that *Things Will Be Different* emerged and continues to evolve (Lucie, Will and I still meet up to talk politics). But of course, thematically, it is this principle of relationality that defines the film's content, as public housing tenants support each other through the imminent rupture of their homes and community.

To fully grasp the systemic failures of the new development, it is crucial to understand that the displacement of the former Walker Street Estate public housing residents is positioned within the settler-colonial logic of ongoing Indigenous dispossession. Merri Northcote sits on the unceded land of the Wurundjeri-willam people. In 1835, less than 100 metres from the Estate, this area became the site of what is now referred to as the Batman 'treaty', where John Batman claimed to have negotiated the purchase of nearly half of Naarm from the Wurundjeri-willam people through a fraudulent transaction.[5] At present, Merri Northcote's proximity to the site and its exclusion of any acknowledgment of its colonial history—while simultaneously capitalising on the site's 'natural environment' as a selling point—underscore how the privatisation of public housing is entangled with state structures that continue to undermine sovereignty. Displacement and dispossession, here, cannot be understood as just outcomes of policy failure; rather, they are a part of the enduring violence of colonialism, which relies on the erasure of colonial history to legitimise public housing gentrification schemes.[6]

It is through a similar logic of erasure that the eradication of public housing and the dispersal of its communities are enacted under the guise of 'renewal.' The underlying assumption being that providing housing for low-income communities is conditional. But this is not a new phenomenon. It is part of the state's enduring process of systemic neglect in relation to public housing, for which they have failed to provide adequate maintenance over the years. While there is no question about the fact that some of the buildings require elements of 'renewal,' the integrity of their designs is worth considering within the context of redevelopment. This is supported through feasibility studies carried out by OFFICE—a local not-for-profit design and research practice and members of the SPHC—who provide detailed insights into how existing public housing designs could be refurbished without displacing the community.[7]

The functionality and longevity of the former Walker Street Estate have their roots in a period after the Depression, in which urban renewal initiatives (such as the Slum Reclamation and Housing Act 1938) were backed by the belief that providing housing was a responsibility of the state.[8] Walker Street Estate, like many of the walk-up estates built in this era, embodied the Modernist maxim, 'form follows function' and was characterised by a postwar, 'made-to-last' mentality. The arrangement of the buildings had been mapped out in such a way as to position them around a central open area. This orientation meant that front doors were accessed from within the Estate, making incidental interactions possible.

The large central area within the complex consisted of a playground, barbeque area and community garden. These factors incorporated a range of prosocial spaces and mechanisms that encouraged and underpinned a sense of community throughout the Estate. In this sense, the design *worked* because it was built to meet the relational needs of its residents and, in doing so, acknowledged the relationality of community itself. The Merri Northcote redevelopment, by contrast, is justified by the sterile gentrification of a public housing community to enable the accumulation of private. The Homes Victoria website asserts that the redevelopment project is "not just about delivering more homes – it's about building a community."[9] Yet, it is precisely community that is dismantled in the process.

A consultative committee was established to include residents in the new design, but the fact that only one resident, Will, attended is indicative of a process that failed to meaningfully enable community participation. Despite promises of a right to return for former Walker Street residents, their new homes ultimately reflect the interests of a profit-driven market. Merri Northcote's sleek marketing campaign emphasises sustainability, resourcefulness and community, along with its proximity to the Merri Creek, but the actual configuration of the new buildings calls into question the equity of these features for all of its residents. The new estate comprises six buildings: five privately owned buildings and one community housing building managed by a private not-for-profit organisation Housing First. The private buildings overlook the Merri Creek, whereas the community housing complex is oriented towards the border of High Street and appears to be both taller and more compact. Although shared spaces such as the 'piazzas' (which simply translates to 'open squares') have been promoted as community spaces in the marketing campaign, the exclusivity of resident rooftop gardens, restricted to each building's tenants, will confine social interaction between *all* residents to either the piazzas or basketball court. Unlike the original PHRP proposal, which framed the renewal as being tenure-blind through a 'salt and pepper' integration approach that aimed to integrate subsidised housing and private dwellings, Merri Northcote's division is reflective of a broader architectural strategy that maintains separation between social housing and private tenants, with separate buildings, entrances, car parks and outdoor areas.

Above: Merri Northcote Piazza, 2025, photograph by Celeste de Clario Davis.

Love, relationships and community are not abstract ideals; they occur within and are shaped by physical space. The architecture of a place has the capacity to define a range of possible social outcomes. It can enable connection or hinder it entirely. Similarly, methods of documentary-making are never neutral. Documentary approaches that claim to only observe assume a detached position and thus theoretically have no impact on participants. But in doing so, they offer nothing to the relationships and communities they depict. When a process does not account for its relational dynamics, the work risks finality. A building may be cutting-edge in design, yet if it fails to support the relational needs of its residents, its purpose will ultimately be undermined.

It is clear that the so-called Public Housing Renewal Project (PHRP) was never concerned with the regeneration of public housing. From the outset, the privatisation of public housing has only exposed its underlying logic: capital accumulation predicated on the erasure of history and the disposability of public housing residents (even though these are the very communities that make public housing sites appealing to gentrifiers). Merri Northcote's architectural and spatial reconfiguration only reaffirms this logic. Its design does not integrate or include community; it facilitates the emergence of a new, privatised precinct, marketed under 'progressive' rhetoric while denying low-income renters any meaningful voice in its pretext. What's more, if the design process had been informed by a relational understanding of the existing community's needs, Merri Northcote's marketing would not need to draw from the optics of inclusivity. Instead, it would be structured by it.

Relationality isn't too hard to grasp. It occurs all the time and sometimes efforts extend beyond these incidental interactions. As Will muses during his walking tour in the opening scene of *Things Will Be Different*, "I need to convince the developers and the people from the community housing group that it would be better to build an integrated community. I can't convince a company, I can only convince some people and maybe if I convince these people, I'll change what they do. Like, I do believe that this is how change is effected."[11]

01 MAB Corporation. *Design*. Merri Northcote. Accessed July 20, 2025. https://merrinorthcote.com.au/design/.

02 Lucie McMahon. *Things Will Be Different*. Digital video, 65 min. 2024.

03 Porter, Libby, and David Kelly. *Understanding the Assumptions and Impacts of the Victorian Public Housing Renewal Program*. Melbourne: The Centre for Urban Research, RMIT, 2019.

04 Nichols, Bill. *Introduction to Documentary*. 3rd ed. Bloomington: Indiana University Press, 2017.

05 Deadly Story, "The Batman 'Treaty' is Signed," accessed July 20, 2025, https://deadlystory.com/page/culture/history/Batman_treaty.

06 Libby Porter, David Kelly, and Priya Kunjan. "Possessory Stratigraphy: Land Title, Dispossession and Housing Crisis." *International Journal of Housing Policy* 25, no. 3 (2024): Titles and recursive dispossession. https://doi.org/10.1080/19491247.2024.2350143.

07 OFFICE. Retain Repair Reinvest–*Flemington Estate: Feasibility Study and Alternative Design Proposal*. Feasibility study and design proposal. October 6, 2024. https://office.org.au.

08 David Hayward, *The Reluctant Landlords: A History of Public Housing in Australia*. Melbourne: Australian Institute of Urban Studies, 1978. 12. https://www.tandfonline.com/doi citedby/10.1080/08111149608551610#tabModule

09 Homes Victoria. "More and Better Homes Are Coming to Northcote." *Big Housing Build News*, February 27, 2025. Accessed June 22, 2025 https://www.homes.vic.gov.au/news/more-and-better-homes-are-coming-northcote

10 Libby Porter, David Kelly. *Understanding the Assumptions and Impacts of the Victorian Public Housing Renewal Program*. Melbourne: The Centre for Urban Research, RMIT, 2019. 7.

11 Lucie McMahon. *Things Will Be Different*. Digital video, 65 min. 2024.

Above: Lucie McMahon, Still from *The City Speaks* (Crawford Productions, 1965), depicting the construction of the Walker Street Estate in *Things Will Be Different*, 2024.

Below: Lucie McMahon, Still of the Walker Street Estate in *Things Will Be Different*, 2024.

AN ARCHAEOLOGY OF THE FUTURE

IN CONVERSATION WITH LINA GHOTMEH—ARCHITECTURE

Lina Ghotmeh

How may architecture lend itself to healing, memory and resilience, articulating the stories of place, human experience and history while remaining truthful to the present and hopeful for the future? For Lina Ghotmeh, this question has informed her practice, with each project a process of research, discovery and care. Inflection *co-editors Charlotte Schaller and Nethuni Sumanaweera sit down with Lina to discuss how architecture can engage with and embrace these nuances.*

In your lecture Archaeology of the Future delivered as part of the Melbourne School of Design Dean's lecture series, you position archaeology as an investigation of the existing to help envision the future. You also mention looking at architecture as constant research of traces from various disciplines that are synthesised into space by creating this fascinating temporal overlap among the past, present and future. Could you elaborate on how you came to this idea and how significant it has been in your practice?

Growing up in Beirut meant always seeing archaeology. Every time a new building emerges, one discovers traces in a city buried more than seven times. It is interesting to see how our ancestors built space.

I became fascinated by this process of digging, tracing and uncovering the past. Archaeology is not necessarily a linear process but about collecting fragments to reconstruct a reality. It is constantly being reconstructed. Being in Beirut led me to become an architect, as I always hoped we could repair the city. I think of architecture as a way of bringing people together. That archaeological process drove me toward a more research driven architecture practice, where I saw architecture as a way of digging into a place and rather than imposing a building, letting form emerge from the place as if it had always been there.

It somehow also solicits the memory and the knowledge of the place, its resources and traces, both physical and metaphorical. It becomes a process of making as well. My practice treats every project as research, questioning the origins of a typology and thinking about the resources of the place, environment and its physical elements. It becomes an investigative process rather than an internal architect-led one.

Left: Image courtesy of Lina Ghotmeh—Architecture.

Right: Lina Ghotmeh—Architecture Studio, Paris, photograph by Lina Ghotmeh.

That distinction between emergence rather than imposition is great. You have discussed how Beirut has been rewritten in the aftermath of the war and noted a certain sense of amnesia, when engaging with sites with such complex histories, how do you ensure your intervention acknowledges rather than flattens these complexities?

Architecture is a field that deals with complexities. It is important to embrace complexity in our lives, rather than shying away from binary thinking such as black and white, good and bad and to recognise it as shades that exist within our lives. Architecture can address complexity and make it accessible through built space, even when a reality seems simple but conceals complex dynamics of economy, politics and social relationships. To incorporate that complexity, history or the social dynamics of the place requires careful listening, investigation and effort to understand the place.

In your experience, in terms of different approaches to cultural heritage—in Poland for example, cities have been reconstructed as they once were; elsewhere buildings depart entirely from what was there previously. How have the approaches to heritage differed when practicing in France than in Lebanon?

Whether you should build something alike or entirely new is a subject question. It is about bridging between past and future. If a city is rebuilt as it once was, it would not respond to the questions of the present. We are bound to use contemporary technology and respond to the challenges of today. Forms cannot be completely identical; in that sense, they would not be truthful to their time.

The constant question is how to be truthful to one's time while acknowledging the past, roots and knowledge. How can the act of building be truthful to the future so that a building can withstand time and remains relevant in its use, by taking in account of how its users may evolve. Time is cyclical, we learn from the past to make the present and the future. I think architecture has a capacity to foster events for users within it. It is our challenge today to adaptively reuse the existing heritage—how do we transform it to make it respond to contemporary use?

In much of your work a connection between Humans and Nature that is present. To what extent do you interfere with nature—is nature something that is designed into your project, or do you intend for it to evolve organically? In other words, do you wish to not tame it?

Humans are a part of nature. The question is how to incorporate the living into architecture. This comes from thinking about architecture philosophically, in the way materials are used and how textures create porosity and relationships to the unseen. We try to create a closeness to the seasons and time, attentive to the passing of time and the magic of the transformations of nature in architecture.

Your mother was an architect. You also have mentioned an interest in biology and genetics—the 'DNA' of the past and how things transform with time in relation to their environment. Could you talk about how these things informed your practice?

Scientists today talk about bodies as being composed of more microbes than human cells. Beatriz Colomina and Mark Wigley in *Are We Human?* talk about how Modernism's hygienic approach erased microbes from the built environment, even though we need them to survive. Their disappearance remains one of the biggest challenges to humanity. I am fascinated by biology, which is linked to climate change and how we evolve. Philosophers like Emanuele Coccia talk about these matters and the importance of art and creativity as a way of surviving.

Left: Brick laying for Precise Acts Hermès Workshops, 2019-2023, Normandy, photograph by Takuji Shimmura.
Right: Precise Acts Hermès Workshops, 2019-2023, Normandy, photograph by Lina Ghotmeh—Architecture.

In the Precise Acts for Hermès, your design was instrumental in reviving a lost and forgotten craft. You have described the act of building as one rooted in love, deeply connected to the environment from which it emerges. In your view, does architecture bear a responsibility to emphasise region specific practices?

It is about allowing architecture and construction to be an act of love, bringing dignity to the environment, the people and the community. It is about building positivity and allowing for connections to happen. I am always thinking about the reconstruction process to build knowledge and to give the hand a role, even with technology, craft remains important. It is about connecting users to place through the materials. Whenever it is possible to revive craft and bring it to the present, it is about that depth of history and allowing it to continue into the future.

I understand there are many different words in Arabic for 'love.' Have the poetics of language and the languages you speak influenced the way you design?

Definitely. Arabic is a very poetic and very metaphorical language. There is a sense of constant layering in the way the language unveils itself and a great tradition of poetry and writing that has influenced my language and my semantics of architecture. This complexity of meaning that is present in every project yet with a sense of accessibility and understanding. It is a simple formal idea with many layers and a lot of metaphors that can be present within a building itself. If you look at Herm s, you see the arches that speak about the span of the brick but also to the gallop of the horses. There is embedded meaning and movement present.

Above: Lina Ghotmeh—Architecture, Stone Garden Housing, 2011-2020, Beirut, photograph by Laurian G.

Could you tell us about the facade at Stone Garden, as it has a fascinating tactile facade that seems so much a part of Beirut.

The idea for this facade was to echo a structure emerging from the ground almost like a vertical ground. It also echoes forms in Beirut like the Pigeon Rock, the seaside landmark that has withstood so many events that have happened. Echoing that natural form became a way and a pretext to make brick part of the architecture. By allowing the facade to be sculpted by artist's hand and by the many people who were involved. There were a lot of scenes at that time with the instability of the war.

The process of making the building became emotional, as it became an experiment of working together while we figured out how to chisel the facade. The idea was to bring this plaster and coat the facade with a thick layer, three centimetres deep and to comb it with a metal three-metre-high comb by hand.

I am interested in this occurrence when spaces are used in ways different from their original intent. Could you talk about this happening in your projects?

From the beginning of my practice, I was interested in the question of 'uncertain space:' an interest in situations, movements and how we can imagine a framework for an event, after which something happens without anyone really controlling the program or user's function in the space. Architecture can generate events but does not dictate what happens. So, there is a sense of freedom in the way one can use the space. At the Estonian National Museum, the main hall, an open space between the shop, library and exhibition spaces, is defined by the incoming light. It becomes a space that can be used, like a human bridge over a lake, an intersection between the theme of the exhibition and the library's activities, so another event can happen there; a site for serendipity.

You have mentioned Beirut's exaggerated sense of life and celebration amidst uncertainty. In light of today's global challenges, whether it is geopolitical or climate change, where do you see architecture and the practice of design fitting in? What role do you think architecture plays in the world today?

In a time when we are surrounded by a somewhat gloomy, often negative environment where we see wars or climate change accelerating without action, even when taken seriously by governments, architecture is a spur of hope. It is an active discipline that allows us to critically assess these dynamics and shift them to create a positive impact and generate opportunities for change even at a small scale. It is a way of being resilient, a way of changing and questioning the status quo constantly whatever the impact might be.

In the design for Stone Garden, all the windows and openings are a critique on what you call the "mushrooming" of new developments in Beirut. Could you talk about architecture as a mechanism of healing, or an expression of individuality against the mass-produced?

It is about allowing individuality and action. After traumatic events, we rush to reconstruct the destroyed spaces or create memorials. They are very passive spaces that you just visit. I am interested in how a memorial can become an active space. Through this participation, a connection happens, a healing process. In Stone Garden, the fact that each apartment is different is about empowering the user to be able to occupy the dwelling and transform it. And because all the openings and loggias face nature, it is about bringing life in, allowing life to be part of that building and of those forms, which were once were snipers holes in the buildings.

In other projects, such as the Osaka Pavilion, it is also about how to respond to environments of temporary construction and sometimes aggressive contexts of fast construction, by making a building that allows breathing space, is open to the environment and is even built to be unbuilt. By an act of modesty and by possibilities of lightness and simplicity that encourage well-being, even in environments that can be violent to experience.

You've been very bold in your career. At 26 you won the competition for the Estonian National Museum, for young architects, could you tell us how this went from a paper proposal to your largest built project to date?

I started my practice at Jean Nouvel's office and Foster + Partners. After two years, I found this museum competition and I invited two other colleagues to join. I was always looking for competitions and projects. Estonia has a very traumatic lived history and somehow it echoed what I had lived in Lebanon and Beirut. The Museum's open identity and constant identity-making also interested me at the time, I was interested with sociology and ethnography, rethinking notions often taken for granted. When we won this project, a lot of people said it would never be built; it was an *ideas* competition they believed would never happen. Part of our jobs as architects is really to take risks. I am constantly taking risks. Every project is a risk as you are working with different disciplines and people. You must push for visions to happen!

For the Estonian Museum, upon arriving in Estonia, the clients were very surprised by two things: firstly, that we are not Estonian and secondly that we were very young. It aligned with a moment when Estonia was led by a young generation. The director of the museum, Krista Aru was a great supporter of the project and we had close relationship with her. It took a lot of perseverance to push for this project to happen and at one point there was a risk that it wouldn't be constructed. It is about putting yourself into the architecture. But architecture is not only about learning and studying, nor is it about having your own practice; it is about finding where you can contribute meaningfully, because in the end it is a collaborative practice.

How extensive was the research and site analysis to identify all these elements—for example the cornflower motif of resistance. Did you live in Tartu to pick up on these local details that you couldn't have gotten from only desktop research?

Yes, I was going there every two weeks, so almost living in Tartu. At one point, I told the museum director I saw her more than my mother. The process was about really understanding the culture: visiting museums, festivals, picking up on traditions and really understanding the culture. It was a combination of desktop research and having access to a lot of information and knowledge—a multiplicity of mediums and initiatives.

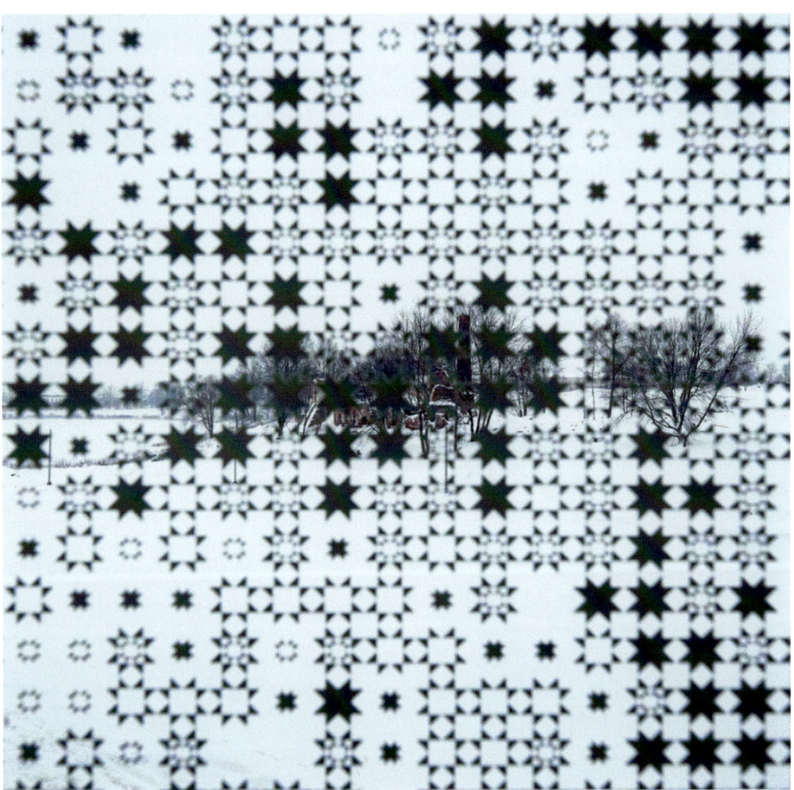

Right: Estonian National Museum, 2006-2016, Tartu, photograph by Takuji Shimura.

I understand the cornflower motif used on the Estonian Museum facade was also a symbol of resistance in Estonia.

Fabric art and knitting are very much a part of Estonian society. It was largely women's work. They would knit the cornflower as a way of preserving their identity without voicing it, to be resistant to the occupation.

Do you have a reflection on love? How might architecture emerge from this?

Architecture is about constantly being in love. In every project you have to be infatuated and be in love with what you're doing—to be able to surmount all of the challenges and difficulties and be blinded!

What advice, then, do you have for younger architects? Is it to be passionate, to be in love or to be bold?

Patience and perseverance. You must work on yourselves as well. It is a challenging time for younger generations because there is a constant flow of information, social media and interactions that offer instant gratification which does not exist in reality. You are not instantly gratified; things take time. You may face more difficulties and challenges than successes, so you need perseverance and grit to keep learning and doing things and believe in things—not to chase instant joy. This applies to knowledge too. There is a difference between having information and having knowledge. Information can be acquired quickly from Google and even worse now from ChatGPT, but it is only one version of things. Knowledge is about research; it is about going deeper into a subject to uncover its multiple facets and not to be afraid of complexity. Allowing this to remain part of ourselves and our humanity, so we can live together, even as we differ. If we do not understand complexity and otherness, we cannot accept the other.

It is like making a model or a project. You build the model and the process becomes a complex journey of assembling materials, thinking about the construction and unforeseeable errors. Working with your hands turns into a process of learning. If you print the project immediately once it is finished it on the computer, you only have one version. Making is about allowing these errors and allowing creativity to happen, letting the imagination be unleashed.

PASSAGES FROM AN ALLITERATIVE LEXICON OF ARCHITECTURAL MEMORIES: A COMPENDIOUS COMPENDIUM

Alberto Pérez-Gómez

The following passages are drawn from Alberto Pérez-Gómez's newly published two-volume opus, An Alliterative Lexicon of Architectural Memories: A Compendious Compendium *(Rightangle International, 2024). This expansive project brings together philological enquiry, historical scholarship and a compilation of personal memories to form a poetic lexicon tracing the history and meaning of architecture. These selective entries unfold in the manner of an architectural dictionary, composed with great erudition and traverse Classical and Medieval, Moorish and Gothic traditions and beyond. Each entry is introduced with a definition—often a familiar architectural term, whose meaning is traced and expanded across time. They are accompanied by a sub-entry, illustrated with small photographs of the architectural sites Pérez-Gómez has encountered throughout his career. Each entry subsequently presents a revisitation through memory. The fragments presented here are but a modest account of the vastly larger compendium, wherein every architectural element—acanthus, aedicule, caryatid, gorge, Rod of Asclepius, scallop—becomes a layered instance of intimate reflection and a reminder of how each detail or element, be it individually or composed within space, imprints itself upon our memory.*

acanthus.

Exalted *ornamental foliage on *astragals and *capitals, enlivening *Corinthian columns. Architectural acanthus mimicking the *acanthus spinosus*: According to legend, one of these plants actively growing, averse to death, blooming around a basket left as an offering over the *tomb of a young Peloponnesian virgin. The affecting scene admired and drawn by Callimachus: Acanthus carved as petrified, surmounting death: *Architecture as anamnesis.

After a lunch of anchovies on bread, wine and apricots, I alleviate an agonising desire by ambling around two Roman circular *temples, one dedicated to Vesta, ancient abode of virgins, the other, a short walk away, victorious Hercules by the river. I add my footsteps with abandon to the round dance of *Corinthian columns, their affecting coiffures astonishingly accentuated by abundant acanthus. Afloat with the wind, I dream that it is time to abrogate Christianity's abolition of the fire, a spark of the Roman sun reflected in my heart, the vestal hearth alight again.

aedicule.

Anglicised from *aedicula*, diminutive of Lat. *aedes*, "house, *temple building." Miniaturised elemental dwelling: vertical *columns or pillars with *entablature and *pediment. Archetypal *architecture transcending *scale: small shrines emulating temples, becoming everlasting models, not unlike *naiskoi*, diminutive of Gr *naos*, "temple, *nave." Extended as metonymic detail: architecture edifying the openings, attentive to the emotional wisdom of divinities: the affecting moods that permeate our pores. Classical aedicules as *niches in temples, freestanding on *pedestals, on domestic *lararia, painted on Greek *vases and on Roman *frescoes, inserted as frames or *niches in stage buildings, thermae, libraries, triumphal arches and *gates, finally as distyle structures making any aperture aediculated. Christian aedicules echoing hallowed omnipresence for cosmic *ecclesia*: Gothic baldachins and elongated tabernacles enveloping sacred statues, framing *altar pieces with more painted aedicules, or enshrining a *reliquary earnestly detailed as a whole edifice. Painted aedicules in Pompeii and Herculaneum: exuberant extensions of domestic space, surrounded by fellow tourists exuding desire. In the *frescoes, the aedicules enfolding represented space and often layered, exacerbating the ambivalent depth of lived *space, as if the geometry were moved by our elated breath. Lines, sometimes arriving perpendicular to the aediculated openings, some converging away as if enthused by horizons, others enthusiastically enticed by our hearts, coming straight to us: the elation of the ebb and flow, vital lan: the endless pushing together and pulling apart that effusively emanates from Eros, present here and now: our entertaining lord and master of enrapturing enslavement.

Aedicules flattened, expanded into solid volumes, elevated and suspended upon ladders and long pillars, fragmented or mutilated: Episodic *emblems used as parody to denote the erasure of enchanted *architecture in the living city. Evident in some Montreal squares and *gardens: the public art of Mel Charney. Exactingly critical yet emotionally feeble as one walks by in daylight, engaging and edifying from a distance when lit up at night: evocative aedicules illuminated like expectant *theatres in dark, effacing environments.

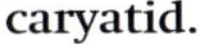

caryatid.

Column carved in the form of a *kore*, Gr. “young woman,” splendidly draped and standing gracefully upright, the ancient ones commonly still held captive in *museums. Caryatids are sometimes conflated with *kanephoroi*, Gr. “basket-bearers,” also commemorated in stone. *Kanephoroi* were young Athenian virgins whose purity confirmed the efficacy of a sacrifice: Appointed to command ritual processions, they marched with cadenced steps, carrying on their heads a *kanoun* containing fruit, a sacrificial knife concealed by barley kernels and festive *ribbons for the consecrated bull. Caryatid columns, all seductive, crystallise divergent stories. Some call to mind Lacedemonian virgins from Karyes, a town between Arcadia and Laconia, who once round-danced in honour of Artemis Karyatis, ecstatically carrying baskets of calamus and undulating as if they were plants coerced into contortions by crazed eudemons. Others, mostly architects, claim that caryatids were women from a treasonous homophonous town that clashed with Athens in some warring conflict and were consequently condemned to carry heavy burdens. Burdens not unlike those of the complaisant *kanephoroi*, who were also responsible for offering honeyed cakes to Athena’s coiled *serpents confined in *cages under the Erechtheion, and who, if they failed in their seduction, foretold countless calamities.

On the *Acropolis Hill stand six comely caryatids, carefully cast copies of ghosts preserved elsewhere, crowned with copious hair woven in tresses like the Cretan *labyrinth and two slender carved *mouldings collaring their headdresses. Concerted, with confident countenances, they carry the *roof of a *porch fronting the Erechtheion, one leg barely forward and the torso very straight, the top curved slightly back, mingling over eons with contrasting cohorts of gods and founding heroes, kings, their concubines, Christian priests and Muslim consorts. The quiescent caryatids appear distinctly captive by the gravity of the *place whenever I have visited under the blinding sun: one winter, the first time, cultivating my solitude and one summer, cavorting with graceful company, the howling of Poseidon's little sea, like Siren's cry, crippling my conscience. But under August's full moon, the caryatids belong to wild Artemis. I have returned under the sensual spell of Seferis, sitting somewhere on the lunar *landscape of Pentelic marble to eat a piece of honey cake: these quirky caryatids take colour from the shadows, heed the call of the goddess and comply: upon the horizontal waves of marble cresting in the clammy fog, they dance as they come forward, emerging from the mist, curling arms upward to carry the sky without effort and night like day they bear my heavy burden.

gorge.

Profiled like a graceful woman's neck, a concave *moulding also called cavetto, from the Lat. "petite hollow," or apophyge, from Gr., "a line in flight," always gorgeous wherever it is found. Associated with passionate throats and narrow passages, from Indo-European -gwora "to devour food," and Latin gurgulio, "wind pipe." Signaling the end of column *shafts, gullets to support their *capitals, or added to combine with other mouldings, as in wavy *cymas. Gorge also turning into its own *ornament as a girdling gorgerin: a seductive *collarino.

The great gorge-*cornices of Hatshepsut's mortuary *temple: a triple horizon built into the desert like a *gate to the afterlife. Old by three and a half millennia and yet eerily modern, expressing timeless enigmas like a De Chirico painting. The temple *plan follows the squaring of heaven: The course of Amun, east-west, towards Karnak on the east bank of the Nile, culminating in the sanctuary of the god, where he can rest and prepare for a new journey, the divine sun kept in motion every day by gifts of food and endless rituals; his course traversing the life cycle of the pharaoh, north-south, a sunny day and a sunless night, life and death and sanctuaries for the glowing Hathor and the gloomy Anubis at opposite ends. Approaching from the east along the causeway, a striking vision emerges: three superimposed *elevations expressing horizontality, their eloquent width divided by a central *ramp; each elevation punctuated by *porticos with simple openings: a staccato of black, slender, pure rectangles framed by limestone the same colour as the desert, set on simple but vast *terraces against the dramatic cliff of Deir-el-Bahari. A temple to glorify life in the realm of the death: the queen's poetic gambit to gain an unending presence. Under scorching sun we advance and slowly climb, her effigies, goals and achievements, sacred statuary and *frescoes, all conventions galvanised by her distinctive ground-bound vision. Hatshepsut's temple rests and rises, its strong gorge-cornices lithe and poised, deflecting the horizon upward, backward; the grand burden of eternity granted the lightness of being.

Rod of Asclepius.

The staff carried by the god, son of Apollo, treading at the limits between life and death. His name meaning "to cut open," rending evil out of dreams. Asclepius the redoubtable oneiric surgeon, his presence a reminder of the miracle of health. A non-poisonous *serpent wrapped around the rod, rightful *emblem of medicine and healing. Readily confused with the *caduceus of *Hermes. Walking across the covered *bridge in Lucerne, a warm summer afternoon. Rambling through medieval *fabric, we come to the Weinmarkt Square, known as the *site of many mystery plays. We are attracted by the *frescoes on the apothecary's *house, above the two lower stories and a small *compass-window, with a date and an inscription: *amor medicabilis nullis herbis*. We translate the Latin, riddled with surprise, "love cannot be cured by any herbs:" The wisdom rendered to Polifilo in his search for Polia, the best, if rare, architectural advice, for desire must always reign. In the centre of the fresco, resting on the architectural frame, an uprooted yet fruit-bearing tree with a sinuous reptile wrapped around its trunk, the serpentine tail thickening on top to become the rump of the temptress Eve, demon with voluptuous torso reaching for a golden apple: the Tree of Life becoming the Tree of Knowledge, flanked on the right by a disembodied hand holding mandrake root, hallucinogenic and narcotic pharmakon, poison and remedy and on the left by the Rod of Asclepius, its figure raised from the ground and casting shadows: represented as a rugged club with a coiled blue *serpent. I recline with my beloved by the *fountain and the pillar, sharing chocolate gelato and our last Croatian peach: incarnation of Asclepius' Panacea, his most remarkable daughter, a universal remedy to heal and nurture our rampant longing.

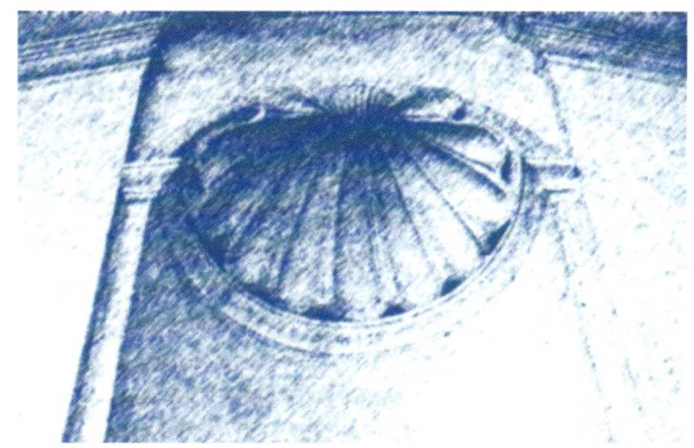

scallop.

From the Old French, *escalope*, symbiosis of *ecail* and *enveloppe*, "scaly covering:" archetypal *shell. Outwardly symbolic of protection, favoured by Christian saints such as Augustin and James; the scallop's serrated armour: *architecture safeguarding faith and chastity in the soul's perpetual struggle with evil. Scallops, like stars, signposting the way for pilgrims to Compostela and on to the last setting sun at Finisterre, signalling salvation at the end of time. Less prudishly, in ancient times, the shell was turned inside out revealing life's inner sanctum: scallops as a symbol of fertility and the feminine principle: the sultry vulva of Aphrodite. Venus Anadyom ne, from An. Gr. *anaduo*, "to surface," the goddess surging out of the sea waves: breaking, spurting surf, seething spume and swollen zephyrs: the smooth naked figure snuggling up to some ivory softness, or standing seductively on the floating shell, squeezing and twisting her long, soaked hair. Scallops in architecture, both pagan and Christian, often found adorning quarter-spherical heads of arched *apses and *niches in Classical buildings, in Baroque *altar-pieces, above *doors, cantilevered over *gates and as balconies like cups, inserted in semi-circular *pediments, portrayed in mosaics and *frescoes and in scalloped *alcoves screening immaculate suspended pearls painted by Piero. Like sensitive, sonorous shells echoing the salty breezes of desire that seize our spirits and stir our dreams, doubling architecture's love and protection, scallops also offer their ambrosia: splendidly raw in nigiri sushi, pan-fried with the zest of lemon, succulent in spicy ceviche or aguachile.

KAI TAK AIRPORT

Greg Girard

Above: Kai Tak Airport–Departures, 1977, photograph by Greg Girard.
Right: Kai Tak Airport–Arriving from Beijing, 1989, photograph by Greg Girard.

You didn't need to be an aviation enthusiast or even a traveller to love Kai Tak Airport. One of the last of Asia's 'downtown' airports, it belonged in a category of its own.

With its single runway sticking into Kowloon Bay, the approach required pilots to note the orange checkerboard painted onto a mountain directly in front of them, disengage the autopilot and then, at 200 feet above one of the world's most densely populated neighbourhoods, make a sharp right turn to line up with the runway.

As the aircraft sliced through its 45-degree turn, passengers on the right side often screamed involuntarily as the right wing dipped down towards apartment rooftops festooned with laundry and television antennae. Then came the hard landings, violent braking and thundering reverse thrust. Welcome to Hong Kong!

From the ground, the spectacle played out with equal drama. The sudden silver underbelly of a screaming 747 would blot out the sky for a split second over the streets and shops crowded with people, close enough to hit with a well-aimed *cha siu bau*. Kai Tak was more than infrastructure; it was part of the theatre of daily life. None of this was planned. As with so much of Hong Kong and as with the best of what made it great, adjustments were made to accommodate limitations of geography, space and an unknowable future. The most perfect example of this played out nearby in the Kowloon Walled City: 35,000 people packed into more than 300 interconnected high-rises, built without architects, engineers or civic administrators.

In a rare example of government intervention, a thirteen-storey height restriction on buildings on the Kowloon Peninsula was strictly enforced. When owners tried to add an extra storey to their buildings, the Urban Services Department would turn up with a police escort and dismantle it.

The Walled City was demolished in 1992. Kai Tak Airport closed in 1998. I made these pictures not for the record or posterity but because, in a place like this—what's not to love?

Following pages:
Kowloon Walled City Rooftop, with 747 approaching Kai Tak Airport, 1989, photograph by Greg Girard.

Homework on Kowloon Walled City Rooftop, with Cathay Pacific Tri-Star approaching Kai Tak Airport in background, 1989, photograph by Greg Girard.

Above: Private high school students - Kwun Tong breakwater - Kai Tak Airport Runway in background, 1987, photograph by Greg Girard.

Above: Cathay Pacific 747 landing at Kai Tak, 1989, photograph by Greg Girard.

Above: View of Kai Tak Airport, with Hong Kong Island in the background, 1992, photograph by Greg Girard.

Left: Aircraft navigation beacon on hill above Shek Kip Mei, 1985, photograph by Greg Girard.

PARLIAMENT (BATH)HOUSE

Iggy Licup

The Parliament (Bath)House is programmatically defined by the bath house and the love room. As a typology, the bath house is deliberately casual and when set against institutions such as the Parliament House, the Old Treasury Building or the Anglican Church in Melbourne, Victoria, it begins to disturb the existing politics of Spring Street. Within the cradle of water, steam and sweat, one feels simultaneously present and removed from the bustle of the public domain. Civic in scale but personal in its offerings, the proposal both agitates *the voyeur* and tranquillises *the occupant*. While it stands as a physical memorial to the customs of love, it raises the question: should the site of Parliament House remain dedicated purely to the impenetrable mystique of Australian politics? Isn't love a form of power and even at times political power?

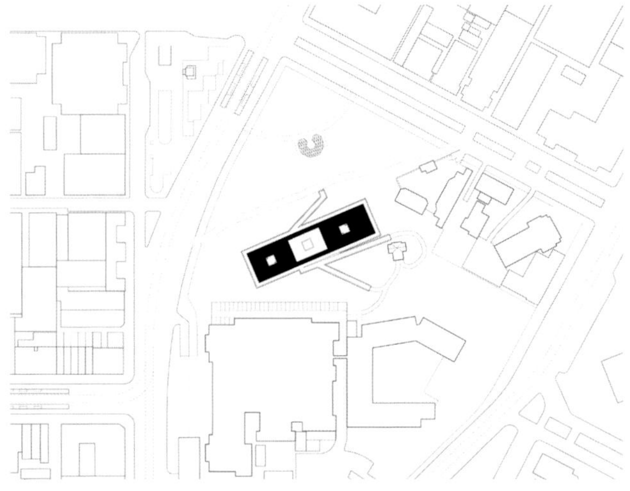

Above: Context plan, 2024 drawing by Iggy Licup.

How does one begin to materialise something as abstract as love? Perhaps by turning to its most immediate object of affection: the body. We first encounter oxytocin, its rush or absence, before the mirror. To manipulate love's chemistry through therapeutic practices is as ancient as prayer: if I love my body I must take care of it. The sauna dilates the blood vessels; the muscles relax. The cold plunge constricts the blood vessels; the senses sharpen. Our internal physiology is therefore subjected to temperature's consequence. The empirical benefits are undeniable; clearly the Romans were onto something.

We can then conclude that love is simply a matter of science.

The Bathhouse entrance is tucked into the landscape of Parliament Gardens, set behind the Pastor Sir Doug and Lady Gladys Nicholls Memorial. Parts of the iron fence that separate the public from Parliament are removed, a discreet gesture visible to the attentive eye. Frosted glass across the facade, disfigures bodies into mere shapes and shadows. The voyeur's gaze is drawn further in.

Once inside the bathhouse, one oscillates between spatial compressions and expansions as programs increase and decrease in scale, dilating and constricting like a human body. Courtyards lead into rooms, then to smaller courtyards and into smaller rooms.

The addition of love rooms is inspired by Japan's notorious love hotels. To ignore the bodily realities of these spaces would be a disservice to the aspirations of a proposal such as this.

In plan, these rooms withdraw to the furthest and most private edge of the site. Their thresholds flanked by four-metre concrete retaining walls, recall Melbourne's seedy midnight laneways. Chance encounters, the flush of skin and as little between bodies as possible—these are the pertinent ingredients to the makings of love within a space.

In essence: *SEX IS PRESENT.*

Above: Sequence 1, 2024 , render by Iggy Licup.

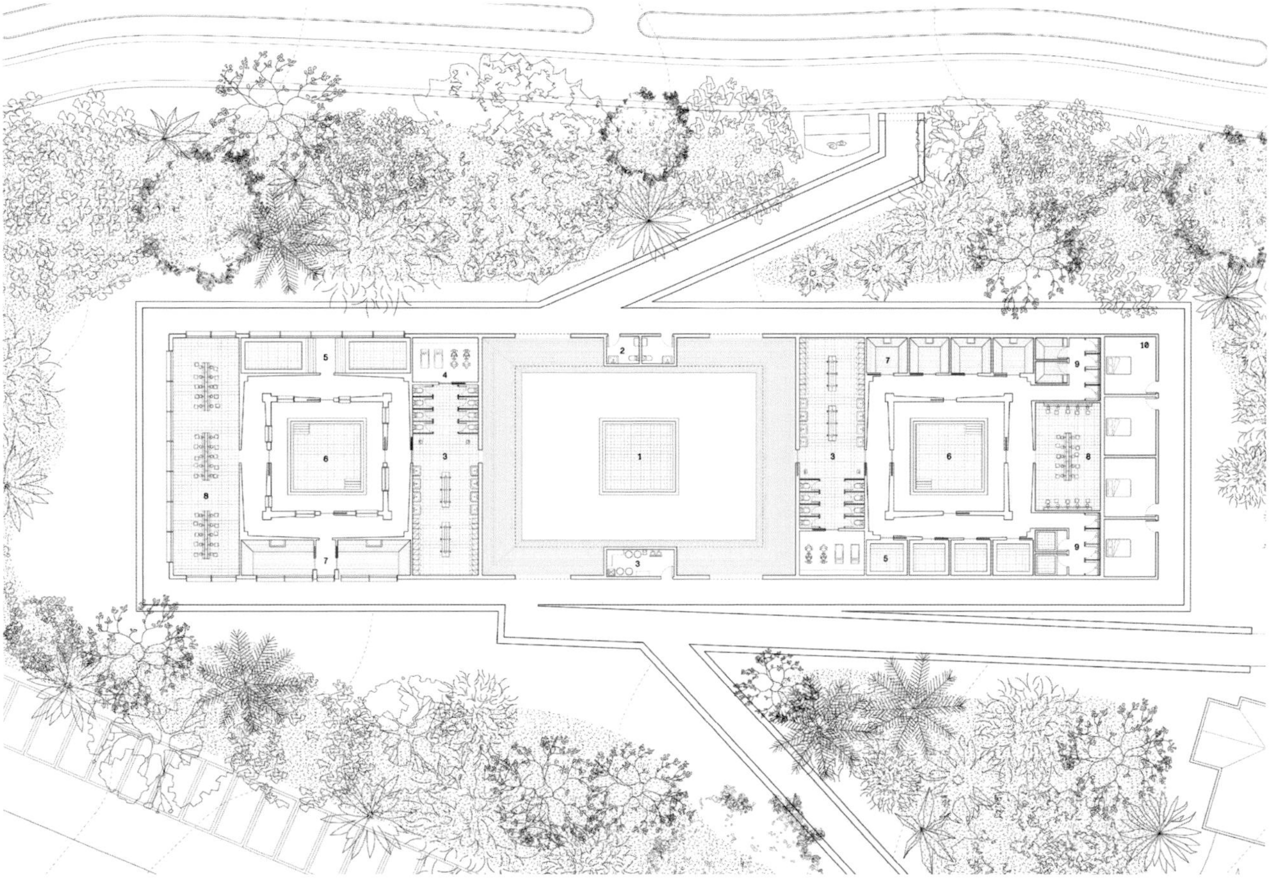

Above: Ground floor Plan, 2024 drawing by Iggy Licup.

1 Main Courtyard
2 Accessible toilets
3 Locker room
4 Gym
5 Cold Plundge
6 Internal Courtyards
7 Sauna
8 Shower room
9 Personal showers
10 Love rooms

Above: South Elevation, 2024 drawing by Iggy Licup.

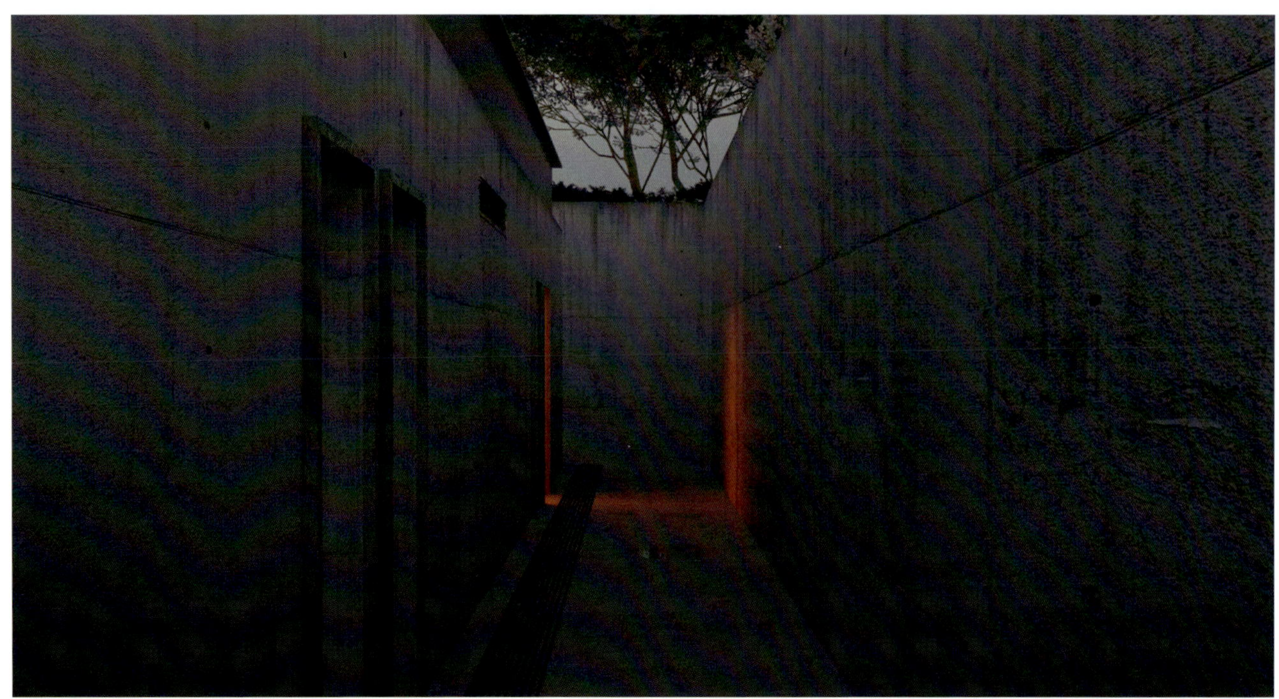

Above: Sequence 2, 2024, Melbourne, render by Iggy Licup.
Below: Sequence 3, 2024, Melbourne, render by Iggy Licup.

Love Hotels

Due to Japan's general conservatism towards the taboo, practices such as casual sex are pushed aside into the shadowy corners of its culture. This in turn manifests as spaces saturated with the aggressively bizarre and the absurd. Love hotels reflect an intersection of cultural attitudes towards privacy, intimacy and customs that are uniquely Japanese.

The specifics of this typology are simple: minimal staff interaction, windowless facades and rooms that become playgrounds for imagination. Nestled within the confinements of the stronghold, one is anonymous but free, choosing among a variety of themed rooms, typically dressed in hyper-caricatures of pop-culture aesthetics. The over-indulgence of ornament is often feminised and by extension we can assume that sexual curiosity (by virtue of love hotels) must be situated within the 'transgressive exploration of forbidden spaces.'[1] These are forbidden spaces that elicit the curious occupant. Pandora and her Box, the Shamed and his Hotel.

If Modernism was about truth, the love hotel, as an agent of Postmodernism, is about fantasy.[2] They are adorned not only to distract the user from the fidelity of the construction, but also to draw the individual away from self-examination. Its glossy red paint conceals the aging of plaster, the weight of shame and the surrender to longing. One whose eyes are titillated by the gloss simply cannot reckon with their unsettled internal states. Minimalism was made for contemplation; its antithesis, for hysteria.

To debate on the Love Hotel's necessity is futile. It offers a retreat from public life. In a culture of structure, tradition and politeness, its existence seems inevitable. This project pursues that very instinct. Who are we to blame the curious citizen for an appetite his culture cannot satiate?

The Love Hotel is symbolic of an object that resists the dominant lifestyle.

Like its Japanese counterparts, The Parliament (Bath) House is dressed in fantasy, it does not shy away from the contradictions of the no-tell motels. Yet beyond its velveteen walls lies a universal truth that transcends politics—here, love, in all its forms, persists.

01 Elizabeth Wilson, "Sexuality and Space," *Harvard Design Magazine*, no. 41 (2015), https://www.harvarddesignmagazine.org/articles/sexuality-and-space-edited-by-beatriz-colomina/.

02 Gerard Rey Lico, "Architecture and Sexuality: The Politics of Gendered Space," *Humanities Diliman* 4, no. 1 (2007): 1–29.

LOVE IS A SCULPTURE BY ROBERT INDIANA

Garry Emery with Jane Mooney

Today we live in an era where truth seems like fiction and fiction seems like truth. We participate in a pluralistic, postmodern era of uncertainty, with challenges such as economic rationalism, anti-neoliberalism, climate change, artificial intelligence, migration, racism, inequity, injustice, political and social conflict, social media, fake news, poverty, the Russian invasion of Ukraine, the Israeli war in Gaza, the United States and Israeli attack on Iran and now Syria, as well as the one-percenters.
All the while, Donald Trump is notoriously—perhaps mindlessly—disrupting the global geopolitical landscape, creating an uncertain, multipolar world with the potential for disastrous consequences.

Where in the world is love? What does love mean and to whom? There have been endless attempts to define what love is. These definitions make more sense when taken together as a collection of different viewpoints rather than as standalone statements. Alone, they are rarely interesting, invariably narrow and personal and unsurprisingly romantic and sentimental. A universally accepted definition of love would not be helpful, as it could be nothing other than confining. Love inevitably means different things to different people.

Pop artist Robert Indiana, best known for his iconic LOVE image, first created this renowned motif in red, green and blue for a MoMA Christmas card that acquired popular recognition as a lowbrow, somewhat trivial marketing communications device.

When Indiana later redefined the motif as a 'work of art' rather than a design, he applied it across numerous art prints and sculptures. These works were exhibited nationally and internationally, establishing an immediate global reputation for the artist and for the LOVE motif.

At the same time, Indiana became the focus of the Gay Liberation Movement after disclosing that the catalyst for his famous LOVE motif was the end of a romantic relationship between him and Ellsworth Kelly—a highly regarded modernist, hard-edge abstract artist and one of Indiana's foremost influences.

Left: Robert Indiana, *LOVE*, 1967, The Museum of Modern Art, New York/Scarla, Florence.
Right: Garry Emery with Jane Mooney, *LOVE*, 2025, A new generation (appropriation) of Robert Indiana's LOVE motif.

To increase awareness, Indiana translated the motif into three additional languages. He recast the individual design compositions to accommodate the unique characterisation of the word 'love' across the planet. This resulted in novel versions in Chinese, Hebrew and Spanish, while maintaining visual recognition and alignment with the original English-language version. The simple, easy-to-comprehend message resonated with the world's conscientious youth and it was soon adopted as a symbol of the Peace Movement. The purpose of the motif diversified, as did its meaning.

Instant fame significantly impacted Indiana's life and career, as both a positive and a negative force. The singular image that brought him widespread global attention became confining, overshadowing his other works. This ultimately prompted him to distance himself from the art world and the overwhelming criticism he received from elite art circles. The image attained and maintained a ubiquitous presence in popular culture and in international Pop Art circles. In today's lexicon, it could be argued that the LOVE motif unintentionally evolved into a highly effective cultural brandmark, a flexible communications device with multiple interpretations determined by its context.

From that point of view, it is difficult to imagine how the motif could possibly have been more effective. Yet, from a fine-art perspective, the motif's inherent populist characteristics were thought to compromise its artistic merit and erode its cultural value. Some critics even questioned its relevance and historical credibility as fine art.

Indiana's 'LOVE' motif is configured within a square format, with stacked slab-serif letters and the letter 'O' tilted on its axis. This unique interpretation of an irreducible, universal theme became a hallmark of the Pop Art movement. Notably, Indiana's first large-scale public sculpture was fabricated in Corten steel, a material commonly found in contemporary architecture.
It has been suggested that there are three main components contributing to the makeup and meaning of the word 'love:' that of passion, intimacy and commitment. Passion stands out as the core component, for without passion an artist, architect, or designer would be unable to develop the mastery needed to make a significant cultural or social contribution. Moreover, to be truly effective, impetuous passion must be embraced with the understanding that as an emotion, it is near impossible to control; passion will inevitably make the artist, architect, or designer too vulnerable. Therefore, to maintain composure and dignity, a passionate emotional condition is best kept completely concealed.

We are living in increasingly uncertain and dangerous times. The legacy our children are destined to inherit is almost unthinkable. Meanwhile, autocrats across

the planet increase their wealth, influence and power, reminding us of the absence of love, tolerance and respect. While the Information Age may have brought us closer together, it has also amplified our differences. That said, in the interest of contributing to a better world, we have developed a new generation (interpretation) of Robert Indiana's LOVE motif, intended for random exposure wherever there is an online opportunity or an unoccupied urban space.

Our aims and our credibility may be questioned, since we are designers rather than artists. We anticipate that, in putting forward this idea, we may be seen as 'getting ahead of ourselves.' While appropriating Robert Indiana's LOVE motif, there is potential to benefit from the cultural currency generated by the fame of the original. The motif is recognisable while deliberately avoiding replication of his design to prevent any potential claims of plagiarism or misuse of intellectual property.

Design and Communication

This project is an appropriation—a visual reinterpretation or 'new generation motif.' The typeface, colours and design compositions have been modified to reposition the image within a contemporary context.

The objective is to capture the zeitgeist—to engage and motivate the public to demand a better, more democratic world for their children. The work maintains respect for Indiana's original artworks. The approach aims to preserve the spirit and general distinguishing features of Indiana's original, while leveraging the currency of that original. This reinterpretation of Robert Indiana's LOVE motif is not intended for commercial gain.

All six sides of the 'digital cube' are programmed to respond to the rhythm of amplified music. The word 'love,' displayed on opposite sides of the cube, will deconstruct and reconstruct through changeable, modular, coloured graphic patterns (see diagrams). The remaining four sides will feature dynamic abstract patterns.

The concept is to play music with a 'peace versus war' message, such as Neil Young's 2010 'Love and War', which may resonate with those who remember the 1960s Civil Rights Movement and opposition to the Vietnam War, interspersed with contemporary music aimed at youth culture, such as US rapper Macklemore's 'HIND'S HALL' on Palestine, to reflect today's issues.

Design modifications to Robert Indiana's LOVE motif by Garry Emery with Jane Mooney.

Below and Right: Garry Emery with Jane Mooney. Proposed new generation (an appropriation) of Robert Indiana's LOVE motif for application to artists prints, dynamic digital sculptures and online communications that will incorporate animations.

LOVE

LOVE

LOVE

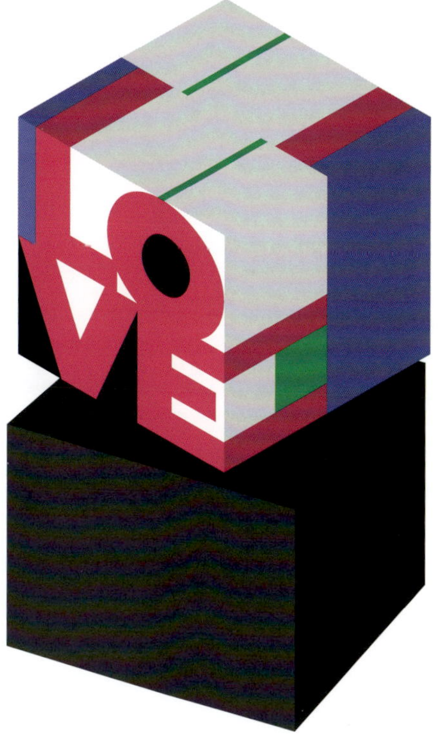
LOVE

HOME AS COUNTRY

IN CONVERSATION WITH THE DESIGN COLLECTIVE OF THE 2025 AUSTRALIAN VENICE BIENNALE PAVILION

Bradley Kerr & Kaylie Salvatori

Jack and Mossy started a Whatsapp group and started chatting to a few of us about possibly putting together a deadly blak team. Our first meeting was actually the day my second son, Oscar, was born and about two weeks before Kaylie's youngest was born. We were just talking about this idea that we don't share stories about home—or what home means to us—very often. I was sitting in the courtyard of the hospital with a 12-hour baby Oscar in my arms, sharing stories about growing up and living with my nan, my grandparents, of my parents taking us to the beach at every opportunity (despite growing up in a very cold Canberra). It was lovely having the time to have such a casual yarn—and I guess we wondered how we enable those types of conversations on somebody else's Country.

- Bradley Kerr on the origins of *Home as Country*

What does it mean to design for home, when the site you are designing for is entirely foreign to you? This was the provocation of the first all-First Nations design team for the Australian Pavilion at the 2025 Venice Biennale. Inflection *co-editor Dorothea Yannoulidis spoke to Bradley Kerr, Quandamooka man and architect working and living on Wurundjeri Country and Kaylie Salvatori, Yuin Budawang woman and landscape architect working on Gundungurra-Dharug Country, about the pavilion and their views on the role of love in design.*

In Australia, as First Nations practitioners, you are often working on someone's Country that is not your own. As non-Indigenous designers, we are always working on someone else's Country. This idea was particularly relevant for the pavilion, located in Venice. How did this factor play into your conception of the exhibition?

BK: I suppose you always want to be mindful of the materials you use, how they're obtained and what happens to them when the project is 'finished.' It was so important not to impose a false sense of Australiana but rather be aware of the fact that we're in Venice. Our proposal was much more about the unique things that we as a collective of First Nations design practitioners could bring to a place that nobody else could. I think one of the beautiful ideas that we had was that if the project were to be rebuilt to tour Australia in 2026, the materials for the rammed earth could be taken from a place of appropriate cultural significance (in conversation and approval of community and elders, of course) and then, when the exhibition finished, the materials could be returned to Country. Materials having a second life allows them to carry the stories and memories with them.

KS: For Venice, we looked at how we might apply our own protocols for the design in place and sought to follow them. This meant that things like the inclusion of native (Australian) plants in the exhibition were omitted as we did not know what the knock-on effects of having Australian plants in the Venetian ecosystem could do. In Australia, the introduction of exotic species has been quite devastating and an act of colonisation. In hindsight, we probably could have substituted with Italian species that have similar properties, which would have been an application of a principle that we often advocate for here in our practice, so that was a missed opportunity—but design holds many lessons.

Architecturally, we sought to use local materials that could go back to the local landscape once the exhibit was over, however the deconstruction of the project and timeframes will impact the reality of implementing our collective principles and I think that this is something that our team will need to revisit. Again, being at the exhibit on the ground held many lessons. I strongly advocate for the exhibition materials across the Biennale to be held in a depot for re-use in future years, as the impact on the local ecosystems, the waste burden, is significant.

***Home as Country* was a collaborative project undertaken by the 'Creative Sphere,' led by Creative Directors Dr. Michael Mossman, Jack Gillmer-Lilley and Professor Emily McDaniel, alongside Elle Davidson, Bradley Kerr, Kaylie Salvatori and Clarence Slockee. Architecture as a discipline is inherently collaborative, yet architectural pedagogy continues to perpetuate the myth of the lone creative genius. The perpetuation of this myth is particularly evident in the case of the Biennale, where generally only one artist or practitioner is invited to represent a nation each year. This year, the Biennale's theme—Intelligens. Natural. Artificial. Collective, envisioned by lead curator Carlo Ratti—prompted consideration of the collective.**

Sarah Lynn Rees in an interview with OFFICE for *The Politics of Public Space* series noted that "Indigenous architecture projects are equally about (if not more about) the relationships and process undertaken during the design process, and the design outcome." We see this manifest in Home as Country. Can you tell us about the process of collaboration and why this was important to the pavilion's development?

KS: In my experience, it's the growth and relationships, making connections and fulfilling obligations to community and Country that give meaning to the process. Whilst design can be about individual expression, I feel I enjoy the process of design a whole lot more when there is collaborative exploration of ideas, friendships made and relationships established. Culturally speaking, we are obliged to ensure that we honour relationships, which is probably why we tend to be more collaborative and less concerned with the outcome (and who gets to hold the pen). If the parameters of the design are established collectively and genuinely—with love—then the outcome should be good anyway. Design outcomes are just one moment along the timeline.

Can you describe for readers the physical character of the pavilion and a little about the process of its construction?

BK: The pavilion was centred around the Round, a rammed earth wall that tapered into a seat and contained the Ceremonial Grounds—a layer of Venetian sand treated with water from both the canal and from home. Surrounding the Round was the Living Cloak—a tapered plaster wall on a plywood frame. Over 140 custom panels were poured by us, the collective and their friends and families. Within a niche in the living cloak lay the students 'Living Belongings'—a collection of models that represented different students' representations of their connection to their culture and to their home. It was important that the exhibition made space for knowledge sharing with younger generations. Plus, I mean, how sick would it be to be a student and have your work shown as part of the Venice Architecture Biennale?

The Venice Biennale is recognised internationally as one of the most prestigious events of the discipline, bringing together thousands of international practitioners and viewed by hundreds of thousands of visitors each year. It has historically been characterised by both the scale of work that it collates and a consistency in the calibre of its exhibitors. The term 'exhibition,' as one might define the Biennale, is charged with historical significance. Its definition usually refers to the presentation of an artefact—a tangible object of prescribed value—that viewers of an exhibit are prompted to passively view. Yet in the case of an 'architecture exhibition,' the definition of what this object might be is less clearly defined. Rejecting the understanding of the exhibition as a passive viewing of one intrinsically valuable piece, *Home as Country* centred instead around a lack of such object: a central, empty, gathering space, created by the rammed earth structure, within which visitors could enter and sit.

The Biennale sits within a long history of artistic institutions which sustain deeply embedded colonial practices: material extraction, destruction, fetishised collection. In her essay, *Choosing the Margin as a Space of Radical Openness* (1989), bell hooks noted: "Home is that place which enables and promotes varied and everchanging perspectives, a place where one discovers new ways of seeing reality, frontiers of difference." Throughout the course of the Biennale, visitors were prompted to sit in the Ceremonial Grounds, engage in discussion and reflect upon other knowledges shared. Amplifying First Nations voices in design through this process, particularly at an international scale, may be one small step towards the decolonisation of such institutions.

Above: Venice Biennale Team, Living Belongings at the Australian Pavilion, HOME AS COUNTRY, 2025, Venice, photograph by Peter Bennetts.

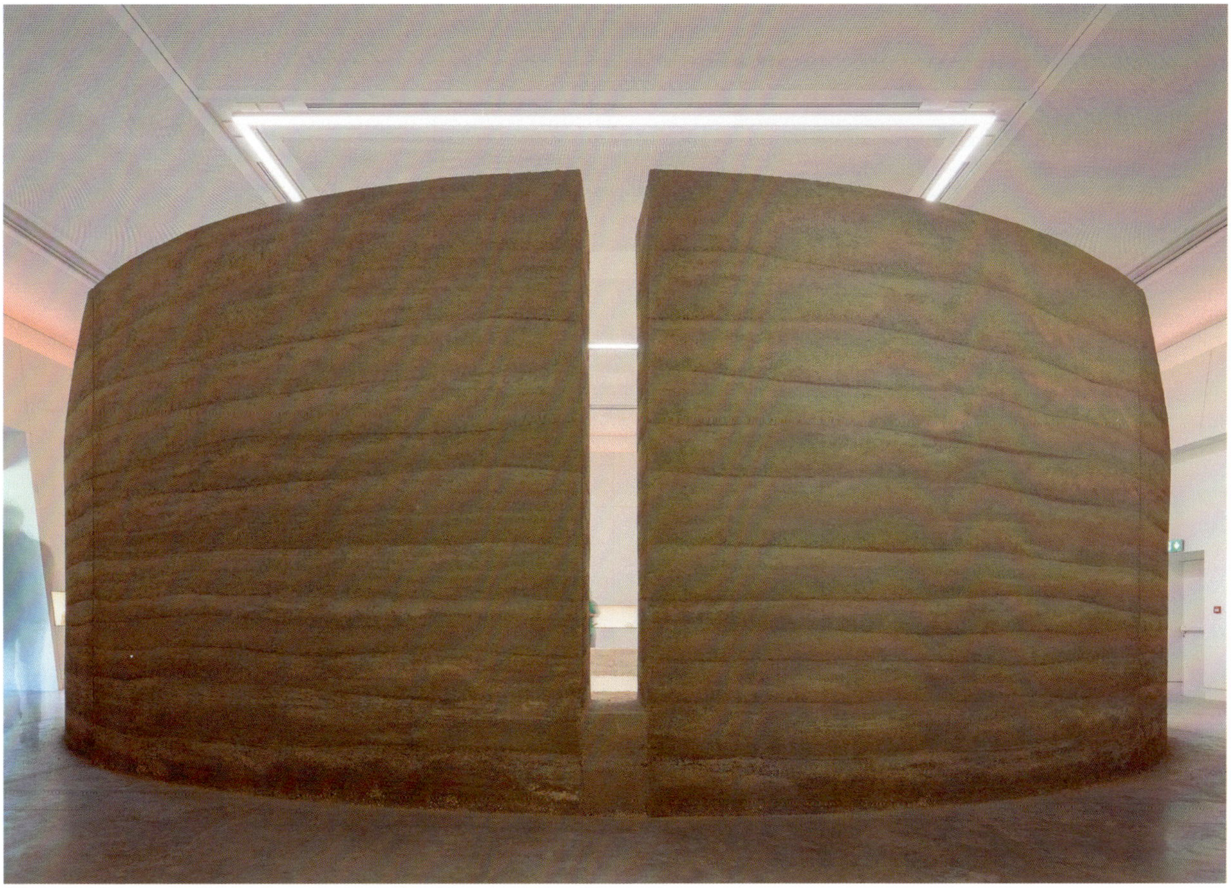

Above: The Round at the Australian Pavilion, HOME AS COUNTRY, 2025, Venice, photograph by Ben Guthrie.

Can you speak to the significance of yarning as an intangible aspect to the pavilion that will live beyond the dissolution of the physical exhibit?

KS: It is hard to decouple this question from my own personal experience. The project lives as a dreamscape in mine and my family's memory, the significance of the yarning and sharing, the actual physical experience of making and the physical experience of navigating a very different place every day whilst working on a project imbued with all of the notions attached to home and belonging. It was a surreal experience. Given the global political context of genocide and war, coupled with the experience of many of the students as immigrants and refugees, working on a project entitled Home in an exhibition that is objectively elitist was an opportunity to re-humanise our collective experiences, hold space and share. But it also held a huge amount of vulnerability; there was significant risk of 'othering' and the spectacle of marginalised experiences that could reinforce paternalistic attitudes of saviourism. This was something we seriously discussed as a collective, which had a huge weight on design and programming decisions. We earnestly sought to emphasise the agency of ourselves, the students and Country, as well as the agency of the visitors in exploring what home means individually and collectively.

BK: I was also adopted into Kaylie's family as my wife and kids were still in Australia. The relationships that you develop when working in that kind of environment are the type of bonds that can last a generation. You see the best and worst and you remember that we are all really human and experience insecurities, fears, hopes and dreams. On the final day before public opening and at the end of judging, I decided to lay-down in the centre of the ceremonial grounds—the sandpit, as we overheard some others call it—and completely broke down in tears. It was hard being there without my family and having no other family join for the opening. One of the proudest moments and you just really want to share it with the people you love the most. Emily noticed, sat with me and we spoke through the fear and the sadness.

Do you see a role for love in the process of the Indigenisation of design?

KS: There is an inherent risk of complicity for First Nations designers—we ultimately walk a tension between change and artifice and often navigate plurality as we try to implement our principles and objectives into a field of practice that has been used as a tool of dispossession for a really, really long time and is still being used as a tool for dispossession today.

Coming at design with love is what shields us from complicity, but it cannot be used naively—just having good intentions is not a genuine application of love. Love requires thoughtfulness, respect, earnestness, care, humility and understanding at a minimum.

The idea of 'home,' being a place embedded with relationships, memories and care, feels intricately enmeshed with the concept of love. How did the idea of love or care sit within the development of *Home as Country*?

KS: Love is embedded within Country and is a definitive factor in relationality. I can't speak to the old ways, but I do feel love as a design driver is very strong for myself and also our collective. We design because of love—love of the process, love of the relationships, love for our Country(ies), love of our Ancestors and Descendants—it is the connective tissue that binds us to where and who we are. Love is understood not just as an emotion but also as act(s), it carries weighty responsibility and duties, it is binding and deep, resonates within us and drives us.

BK: I think love is complex. I'd suggest that home isn't a place of love for everybody. Experiencing unconditional love at home can be quite a privileged thing. Platonic love, love for a child, love for a memory or a place, love for your parents, for your partner, for your dog—they all have a place in parallel with the love of a home and for some, in place of. I think that ensuring the composition of the Round and the proportions of Living Canvas—hand poured plaster panels that took a minimum of 4 people to pour, evocative of imagined landscapes and oceans—were intentionally non-prescriptive. It was so important to us that people did not come in and feel a false sense of Australiana or a false sense of home, but rather that they could take time to find their own place within the pavilion. Every constructed element in the pavilion was built by members of the Creative Sphere. Emily McDaniel put it quite beautifully while we were over there—it's not often that everything in an exhibition gets to be touched, felt or embraced by the visitors—but that's what we all crave—to be touched, to be held, to feel warmth.

What does *Home as Country* mean to you?

KS: *Home as Country*, the experience of the project, represents a surreal dreamscape filled with deep emotions, good yarns and strong relationships that sought to advance in earnestness, the agency of communities, cultures and Country. We held space for everyone to come to the table and discuss with sincerity, humility, joyfulness—and at times, sombreness— about what home means to us, what our connections to place are and what our aspirations for the future are. It morphed as we moved through it, as we built stronger relationships with one and other.

BK: I'm still not certain that it happened, but I know I have long lasting loving friendships with some pretty spectacular people. It was a humbling experience—one that I'll be forever grateful for.

In an exhibition focused on the rise of non-human or artificial knowledges and their role in the development of the architectural discipline today, it might feel contradictory to talk of such a human experience as love. Yet love permeates deeply throughout *Home as Country*.

Above and opposite: Australian Pavilion, HOME AS COUNTRY, 2025, Venice, photographs by Peter Bennetts.

INVITING ACTS OF CARE

ARCHITECTURE'S GIFT

Sarah Robinson

Love is that indescribable glue, the connecting force field that makes nonsense of anything less ultimate. Love reaches into the very heart of architectural meaning. The very impulse to create is an act of love—one of the truest gifts an architect can offer to the world.

Architecture exceeds mere shelter or function; love is the unaccountable factor in sustainability, the other dimension of long-term mutuality in human care. The most sustainable buildings are those that are dearly loved—not only because they are resource-efficient or can be broken back down into parts for future re-use but because they invite the energetic resources of human care across generations. A building that invites care and tenderness in inhabitation, enjoyment and maintenance is not simply a passive beneficiary of these human involvements; by eliciting care it also benefits those who engage with it. For love has not only affective, aesthetic and ethical implications; it is also biochemical and bodily. Failing to acknowledge these interwoven and interacting dimensions impoverishes architectural potential and meaning.

Affective Fields and Resonant Bodies

Love is not uniquely human, but an affective force shared with our fellow animals. Affect, as decades of work in cognitive neuroscience have demonstrated is not something confined to an individual but is shared and situational. We register a situation's affective tenor through the resonance between our bodies and our worlds; our bodies, as William James insisted are the most "sensitive sounding boards."[1] John Dewey understood affect to be a kind of "organic-motor *resonance*" and "a reverberation of organic movements" within a larger coordinated pattern of action.[2] In these understandings, affect and emotions are not discrete internal states of the psyche, nor isolated subjective states bounded by the interior self but an overall objective quality of the situation.

Instead of saying "I am joyful," it is perhaps more appropriate to say that "the situation is joyous."[3] The proper locus of emotion is neither solely in the person nor in the situation but in the interaction between an organism and its environment within a shared affective milieu. As psychologist and philosopher Thomas Fuchs writes, "Feelings befall us; they emerge from situations, persons and objects which have their expressive features and which attract or repel us. This *affective space* is essentially felt through the medium of the body which widens, tightens, weakens, trembles, shakes etc. in correspondence to the affects and atmospheres that we experience."[4]

He terms this process body *resonance*, in which bodily sensations (such as warmth, tension or relaxation) and physical reactions (such as shivering, a racing heart or the tension or trembling of fear that directs us to withdraw) are not so much expressions of emotion as the emotion *itself*. Affect is not confined to the individual but gauges the interaction between person and environment—both of which possess affective qualities. Embodied affectivity involves the whole interactive cycle registered through the resonance of the feeling body.[5] In this process, the hard lines we draw between ourselves and the world beyond our skin begin to dissolve.

Affective Systems

Pioneering neuroscientist Jaak Panksepp demonstrated the biological continuity of affect across species by articulating the seven affective systems that we share with other animals and detailing their neurobiological bases.[6]

Affect is embedded in situational factors and amplified or dampened by them with clear spatial implications. Baby birds are often more connected to their nests than to their mothers. Rats return repeatedly to the locations where they copulated.[7] Researchers working with these subjects observe that they arrange their spaces according to the activities conducted within them. Space, in this sense, is not a neutral backdrop but affords, invites or prohibits certain behaviours. If this is true for rats, birds and ants, how much more so is it for the human animal?

Panksepp's affective systems include the seeking system, associated with exploration, curiosity and the pursuit of rewards; it motivates animals to seek out resources and engage in activities that are necessary for survival and reproduction. The fear system governs responses to danger and threat, triggering defensive behaviours and physiological changes that promote avoidance or escape. The care system supports nurturing and caregiving behaviours, particularly in parental care and social bonding. The panic/grief system is activated by separation from attachment figures or the loss of social bonds. It is associated with distress and longing for social connection. The play system supports social bonding, communication and the development of social skills through playful interaction. Together, these systems interact to ensure the survival and flourishing of the species. To create life-affirming, resonant places, the seeking, care and play systems and an awareness of the fear, panic and grief systems can inform design strategies that protect against and support coping with, these inevitable life processes.

Care, Bonding and Place Attachment

The care system is associated with nurturing and caregiving behaviours, particularly parental care and social bonding. All these interactions take place in and are supported by specific types of environments. It is well documented that people form bonds not only with one another but also with places. Place attachment parallels bonding with others, yet is typically more complex, layered with memories and social experiences. Cherished places ground a sense of identity as loci of affect.

Early childhood places in particular are a primary fabric for the emergence of belonging, becoming a measure against which later experiences are gauged. These places are matrices of care and have a biochemical signature in caring and loving experiences. Care releases oxytocin, the neuropeptide of love.

"Neuropeptides may serve command functions in the brain, helping to synchronise a variety of bodily and brain systems to unconditionally promote coherent organismic responses to primal survival needs," writes Panksepp.[8] Oxytocin's role in maternal pleasure and bonding, sexual readiness and nurturing emotional patterns speaks to its evolutionary significance. Caring involves more than relationships with other humans and oxytocin is released in relationships with animals, plants and the places in which we dwell. Touch releases oxytocin, as does working with microbe-rich soil. Oxytocin induces place preference, which may explain rats' preference for their trysting sites. In non-human mammals, the neuropeptide oxytocin has repeatedly been shown to increase social approach behaviour and pair bonding to reduce social stress and to enhance attachment security.[9]

Oxytocin functions as an anxiolytic, helping to keep calm and regulate stress responses by lowering blood pressure and reducing levels of stress-related hormones during challenging situations. The biochemical release and cascade of positive effects associated with place bonding and attachment underscore the crucial role of place—an amalgam of built, historical, natural and affective components—in supporting relationships of care. These effects are interactive and mutual: caring for places releases positive neuropeptides just as receiving care does. This entails places that harbour life; not only plants and animals, but also life processes (such as ageing and decay) that require human intervention. The act of caring for one's home, garden, park and community releases a cascade of positivity. As architects, it is our role and duty to create places worthy of evoking such acts of care. The most sustainable places are those dearly loved—through caring for them, we ultimately become calmer, kinder and more socially connected.

01 William James, "What Is an Emotion?" *Mind* 9, no. 34 (April 1884): 188-205, http://www.jstor.org/stable/2246769.
02 John Dewey, "The Theory of Emotion: (I) Emotional Attitudes," *Psychological Review* 1 (1894): 553–556.
03 I have used the words emotion, feeling and affect interchangeably here to emphasise their generality and pervasiveness. A full treatment of their distinctions is beyond the scope of this work.
04 Thomas Fuchs, "The Phenomenology of Affectivity," in *The Oxford Handbook of Philosophy and Psychiatry*, ed. K. W. M. Fulford et al. (Oxford: Oxford University Press, 2013), 63.
05 Sarah Robinson, *The Architecture of Resonance: From Objects to Interactions* (Abingdon: Routledge, 2025), 61-65
06 Jaak Panksepp, *Affective Neuroscience: The Foundations of Human and Animal Emotions* (New York: Oxford University Press, 1998), 24-26
07 Panksepp, Affective Neuroscience, 248.
08 Jaak Panksepp, "Oxytocin Effects on Emotional Processes: Separation Distress, Social Bonding, and Relationships to Psychiatric Disorders," in *Oxytocin in Maternal, Sexual, and Social Behaviors*, ed. C. A. Pedersen, J. D. Caldwell, G. F. Jirikowski, and T. R. Insel (New York: New York Academy of Sciences, 1992), 243–252.
09 Panksepp, *Affective Neuroscience*, 255.

CAMPANILISMO AND CARE

ON THE CULTURAL COMPLEXITIES OF ITALO-AUSTRALIAN SOCIAL CLUBS

James Urlini

On 8 August 2025, the Fogolar Furlan Club in Thornbury lost its bid for temporary heritage protection. The Department of Transport and Planning (DTP) acknowledged the club's community significance but rejected the application by the City of Darebin, citing "uncertainties over the continuation of the Club's activities on the land" and the impact of a February 2024 fire on the club's heritage significance.[1] For more than half a century, the Fogolar Furlan Club has been a second home for Melbourne's Friulani, a diasporic community from northeastern Italy—and has become a place of language, recipes, rituals and allegiances to nearby bell towers. The decision by DTP against granting heritage protection is symptomatic of broader issues—namely, how heritage is defined in Victoria, and how little room its frameworks leave for acknowledging migrant histories and ways of belonging.

Let us consider Italian social clubs through two entangled ideas: *campanilismo* and care. *Campanilismo*—literally 'bell tower-ism'—describes impassioned local and regional loyalties. It's why Melbourne never had a single 'Italian Club' but dozens of smaller ones, each tethered to a province, town or local symbol. Care is what has allowed these places to persist—from unpaid cooking, endless fundraising, volunteering and working bees to the quiet daily work of sustaining language, culture and community across generations. These elements form the backbone of an unofficial migrant heritage present in Melbourne and across Australia.

Campanilismo—Building Bell Towers in Suburbia

Campanilismo is a worldview that has long defined Italian belonging—a pride and loyalty to one's local neighbourhood, town or region—measured, as the saying goes, by the reach of its bell tower. While the nation-state remained abstract and distant, the campanile was immediate. For Italians migrating to Australia in the postwar years, regional pride did not dissolve upon arrival but instead grew deeper. Migration fractured existing communities. Migrant reception centres dispersed former neighbours; temporary work arrangements became lifelong settlement; and subsequent chain migrations drew towns abroad. Once here, rebuilding a sense of local community was most familiar at a regional, not national, scale.

This alignment with localism is rooted in Italy's cultural and political history, predating its formal unification in 1861. The former Prime Minister of Sardinia, Massimo d'Azeglio, wrote in a memoir published posthumously a year after the 1866 annexation of the Veneto, "Unfortunately Italy was made, but Italians are not being made," a sentiment later popularised as the slogan, "We have made Italy. Now we must make Italians."[2] For centuries before unification, the peninsula had been divided into several small states, often under foreign dominion or allegiance. Loyalties cohered locally rather than to an imagined national whole, differing so much in "language, social structure and cultural tradition that the maintenance of a local identity [was] an enduring feature of Italian cultural identity."[3] Standard Italian, still consolidating in the twentieth century, imposed itself over Italy's many vernaculars—today recognised as distinct languages—and recast them as 'dialects,' an erasure of linguistic difference that served the project of Italian nationalism. Most Italians were effectively bilingual or trilingual, navigating everyday life through community languages while acquiring a standardised tongue. As Italo Svevo's protagonist Zeno laments, "With every word we utter in Tuscan, we lie!"—capturing the estrangement inherent in the adoption of the national language.[4] Even within Italy, self-expression was mediated by systems that felt imposed and inauthentic. It is unsurprising then that Italian diaspora communities in Melbourne, unlike other European diasporas that maintained culturally nationalistic institutions (Denmark House, the Celtic Club, the German Club Tivoli to name a few) reproduced themselves along local lines rather than unifying under a single 'Italian Club.' The proliferation of regionally oriented clubs reveals the operational logic of *campanilismo* in Melbourne's suburbs. Dozens of distinct communities congregated around common languages, foods and place identities to establish these social clubs, often founded alongside or divergent from associated sports teams—Veneto, Abruzzo, Lazio-Marche, Trieste, Floridia, Calabria, Reggio Calabria, Vizzini, San Marco in Lamis and more.[5] A few pan-Italian clubs did emerge, such as the Williamstown Italian Social Club and the Freccia Azzura Club but these were exceptions. Each of Victoria's forty-odd remaining clubs serves as a reminder to its members of where they came from.

Above: Firefighters at the Furlan Club, photograph by *The Age*.

The dislocation of local peoples is clear in the case of San Marco in Lamis—a town in northern Puglia—from which more than 5,000 migrants arrived in Australia in the 1950s.[6] Today, it is understood that Melbourne's San Marco Lamis diaspora exceeds the town's current population. Demonstrably, *campanilismo* allowed for the reconstitution of intensely localised identities at a global scale. While the 'village' was transplanted into suburban Melbourne, the club grounded its name, dialects, foods, rituals and rivalries in the built environment.

Club buildings are rarely grand and few are architect-designed. It is donated labour, community fundraising and personal financial entanglements that willed them into existence. Former factories and community halls were restructured as places of gathering. Their modest material presence often obscured their cultural significance. Estranged from their homelands, Italian social clubs produced spaces that were 'almost, but not quite, at home,' stabilising a sense of belonging following years of instability.[7]

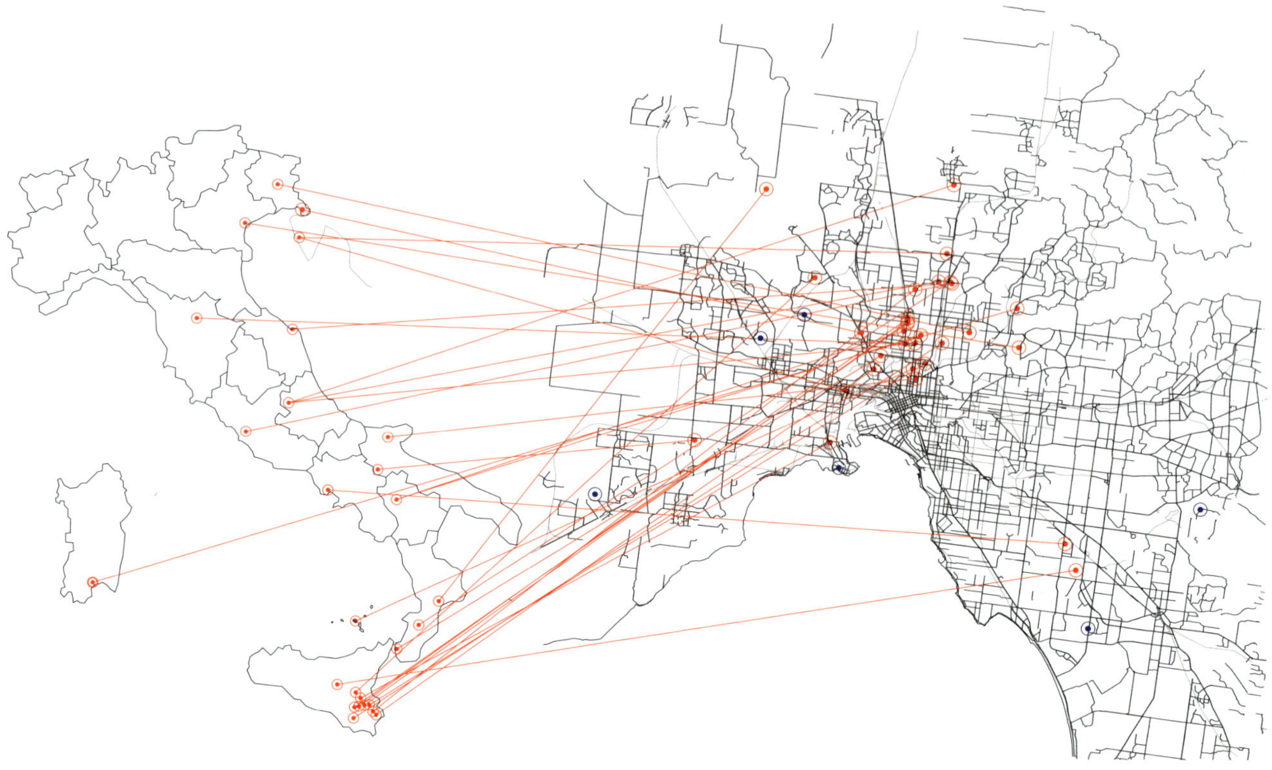

Above: Italian Social Clubs in Melbourne and their associated places in contemporary Italy. James Urlini, 2024.

In this sense, *campanilismo* takes on new meaning. The attachment of the social club to village and region, while deeply cultural, performed a tactical role in grounding the community in suburban Melbourne—declaring that the Friulani, Calabresi and Laziali were here, were staying and had a place of their own. If assimilationist Australia viewed 'Italians' as a singular monocultural migrant group, the clubs reminded members otherwise: they were not necessarily Italian but Pugliesi, Abruzzesi, Siciliani and Veneti. Expressions of *campanilismo* resisted the flattening of identity and carved out spaces of local pride in a foreign anglophone land. The clubs were less about architecture than about allegiance. While *campanilismo* structured their social and material identities, what sustained them across decades, was care.

Care—A Quiet Form of Heritage

If *campanilismo* explains why so many clubs were realised postwar, modes of care explain how and why they have endured. The heritage of these venues is not only built but enacted—through countless unpaid hours spent cooking, fundraising, organising dances, running working bees, coaching soccer teams and hosting weddings and funerals. These clubs provided social infrastructure—shared meals, bocce courts, soccer fields, card nights, bingo, fancy dress, film screenings, English classes and language schools. They were places where language could be spoken without shame or misunderstanding, where children could perform folk dances without mockery. In an Australia that was often hostile or indifferent, social clubs offered shelter against assimilation and isolation alike.

Care often took the form of ambition. Clubs sought larger, more modern venues—through relocation or renovation—driven by necessity and a pursuit of prestige. In 1976, while located on Lygon Street, East Brunswick, the Floridia Social Club commissioned Joe Arcaro of G&J Designs, Oakleigh for a purpose-built clubhouse in Essendon.[8] Following a general meeting in 1979, however, the committee informed the Health Commission of Victoria's Building and Services Division that the project would be abandoned on cost grounds. Soon after, the club relocated to the former Kensington Masonic Lodge in Flemington, where it remains today. Their path—from an initial venue, to architectural aspirations, to a compromise within the

Above: Trieste's Bishop, Lorenzo Bellomi, visiting the San Giusto Alabarda Social Club, Melbourne, 1989. Photograph by Gianfranco Cresciani.

existing building stock—marks a recurrent pattern in the history of Italian social clubs. Such unrealised projects are evidence of ambition, resource constraints and adaptation—each influential to the trajectories of migrant clubs and their interactions with the built environment.

Prestige operated laterally, particularly through inter-club associations. Many regional clubs established federations, reinforcing the expression of *campanilismo* while extending them into forms of soft diplomacy. These connections often linked directly to postwar Italy, with clubs acting as regional embassies that kept alive religious festivals, celebrations of patron saints and official ties with municipal governments abroad. These networks were another mode of care, sustaining identity across distance and time.

Anna Karlstr m argues for the consideration of heritage as a "renewable resource," not fixed but continually recreated.[9] To privilege only intact or architecturally celebrated clubs risks erasing those sustained through adaptation. Research on the 'migrant house' by Lozanovska, Levin and Gantala reinforces this: for many migrants, the act of building was more significant than its final appearance. Construction of these buildings was a communal event sustained by obligation, festivity and food.[10]

Care, then, is the invisible heritage of these clubs. It is not easily materialised nor archived, although traces survive in photographs, plans, news articles and memorabilia. Embodied labour, adaptation, continuity and pride are why these modest spaces matter and have long mattered. Without recognising this, heritage assessments risk erasing precisely what made these clubs significant in the first place.

Crisis—The Limits of Recognition

The refusal of heritage protection for the Furlan Club crystallises the crisis facing Italian social clubs today. The DTP's reasoning, that fire damage compromised its intactness and that the continuation of activities was uncertain, followed the logic of established heritage criteria. Yet those very criteria are the problem. They assume that heritage resides in material fabric and stable use, that significance is fixed at a building's inception and that it endures unchanged. Migrant heritage has never looked like that. It is episodic, contingent, often messy—a factory repurposed, committees formed, deformed and reformed, DIY interiors layered— their spaces made places as they thicken with time.11 To judge significance by intactness is to misunderstand the very conditions of migrant life.

Above: Birthday party at the Trieste Social Club (formerly the San Giusto Alabarda Club), c. 1970. Image courtesy of the Trieste Social Club.

The DTP's refusal comes at a moment of demographic shift. First-generation migrants are ageing or gone; subsequent generations relate differently to regional affiliations and club life. This transition makes recognition of their heritage all the more urgent. These spaces are the last material and social remnants of the communities who first built them—containers of care, struggle and adaptation. As memberships rise and fall, the buildings themselves become crucial material evidence of these histories.

In the case of the Trieste Social Club, whose renovation is a lesser-known project of Triestine migr architect Erminio 'Ermin' Smrekar, the interiority of the club evaded the gaze of heritage assessment.[12] Originally built in 1965 by Bill Millar and Ray Barnard-Brown for knitted goods manufacturer Peka Pty Ltd by 1978 the then-San Giusto Alabarda Social Club had purchased the building and commissioned Smrekar to modernise its interiors.[13] Smrekar made only minimal alterations to adapt the building as the club's future home. He infilled the factory's upper floor sawtooth with a vaulted ceiling structure; shifted the entrance to the middle of the facade from its previous position to the left; updated bathroom facilities; and relocated the stairwell, among other alterations. By prefacing interiority over street presence, Smrekar's design effectively placed heritage in the building's use, rather than its facade—leading to its disqualification from Moonee Valley's heritage listing on the grounds that its "historical connections [were] not well expressed in the fabric."[14] Evidently, the inversive nature of club activity is a condition current heritage assessment processes struggle to see.

The crisis is not only financial or demographic but epistemological. Current heritage practice fails to recognise migrant forms of belonging. Contrary to the values it privileges, of monumentality, absolute continuity, distinctiveness and patriotism, what Italian social clubs offer is different: modesty, hybridity, regionalism and care. Their significance does not lie in championing a 'national story,' rather in resisting it and in carving out community spaces amid cultural turbulence. The demolition of the Fogolar Furlan will be more than a loss of material fabric. It will be a double erasure—first of the building itself, then of the memories and attachments it incubated. Unless heritage practice adapts, broadening to encompass care and culturally specific constructions of identity and belonging, the story of migrant Australia will continue to be told in partial

Above: "Il piccolo vademecum chel'Italia donava ai suoi concittadini in partenza per terre lontane: The little pamphlet that Italy gave to its citizens departing for distant lands," image courtesy of Giusy Buccheri.

Above: The Sortino Social Club, protected by Yarra City Council for its former use as a factory. The contemporary significance of the club's activity remains unacknowledged. 2025, photograph by James Urlini.

form and perspective, privileging what is considered monumental, official and assimilated.

***Buona Fortuna Emigrante!*—Good Luck Emigrant!**

The future of the Fogolar Furlan Club is now a history in the making, as is the fate of dozens of clubs across Melbourne, most born as expressions of *campanilismo* and many sustained through care. While they can be serialised as 'Italian social clubs,' they can and should be considered as independent entities—rhizomatic—produced by similar experiences of migration, loss and nostalgia, though each with their own nuances, memories and archives. These venues are typically not grand but they are loved. They contain the labour of communities who recreated their bell towers in the suburbs—who raised funds, prepared meals and argued over committees, all to reconstruct a sense of belonging.

As Anna Karlstr m has argued, heritage is not fixed but continually renewed—it is a resource which is sustained through practice as much as preservation. If heritage is meant to honour what communities value, then Italian social clubs must be recognised for what they represent: a plural of Italian migrations and migrant heritages of loyalty and care, as formative of Victoria's cultural landscape as any monument or civic hall. The crisis of the Fogolar Furlan is not simply a loss for its community but a challenge to the very understanding of Italian migrant heritage—it is both a warning and an invitation. It warns of what will be lost if heritage frameworks remain tied to architectural prestige, intactness and national symbolism. It invites, however, a more inclusive kind of heritage practice—one that might recognise modest forms of continuity and care.

01 "Outcome of heritage overlay application for Furlan Club," City of Darebin, published August 14, 2025, https://www.darebin.vic.gov.au/About-council/News-and-Media/Latest-news/Outcome-of-heritage-overlay-application-for-Furlan-Club

02 Author's translation from the original "purtroppo s'è fatta l'Italia, ma non si fanno gli Italiani." Massimo d'Azeglio, *I miei ricordi*, (1867): 7, https://archive.org/details/bub_gb_1wJcgmJQallC/page/n31/mode/2up

03 Robert Pascoe, *Buongiorno Australia*, Our Italian Heritage, (Victoria: Greenhouse Publications, 1987):11.

04 The full quote is as follows: "With every word we utter in Tuscan, we lie! If only he knew how we love to recount all the things for which we have a ready phrase, and how we avoid those that would force us to resort to the dictionary!" / "Con ogni nostra parola toscana noi mentiamo! Se egli sapesse come raccontiamo con predilezione tutte le cose per le quali abbiamo pronta la frase e come evitiamo quelle che ci obbligherebbero di ricorrere al vocabolario!", Italo Svevo, *Coscienza di Zeno*

05 Adriana Nelli, "1954, Addio Trieste... *The Triestine Community of Melbourne*" (PhD, Victoria University, 2000), 15. https://vuir.vu.edu.au/15651/1/Nelli_2000compressed.pdf

06 "Pugliesi in Australia | *Memorie pugliese in Australia*" https://memoriapugliesi wordpress.com/pugliesi-in-australia/

07 Sara Ahmed, "Home and away: Narratives of migration and estrangement," *International Journal of Cultural Studies* 2, no. 3 (1999): 331, https://doi.org/10.1177/136787799900200303

08 Florida Social Club, corner of Dunlop Avenue and Ascot Vale Road; Essendon, Other VPRS 7882/P0001, 18333, Public Record Office Victoria.

09 Anna Karlström, "Local Heritage and the Problem with Conservation," in *Transcending the Culture–Nature Divide in Cultural Heritage: Views from the Asia–Pacific Region*, eds. Sally Brockwell, Sue O'Connor, and Denis Byrne, Terra Australis 36 (Canberra: ANU Press, 2013), 153

10 Mirjana Lozanovska, Iris Levin, and Maria Victoria Gantala, "Is the Migrant House in Australia an Australian Vernacular Architecture?" *Traditional Dwellings and Settlements Review* 24, no. 2 (2013): 65–78. http://www.jstor.org/stable/41945724.

11 Mike Crang, "Place or Space?" in *Cultural Geography* (Oxford: Taylor & Francis Group, 1998) 100-119. https://doi.org/10.4324/9780203714362

12 Smrekar's other work includes the Veneto Club, Fishermen's Pier Restaurant in Geelong, Lygon Court Shopping Centre, and the "Clock Tower" development in Carlton.

13 Peka Proprietary Limited Willow Street Essendon; new Millar and Barnard Brown, VPRS 10150/P0000, *Plan 2260 File Red 7478*, Public Record Office Victoria.

14 Context Pty Ltd, *Moonee Valley Herixtage Study 2015* (2016), 18.

A CONGREGATION ON A SLOPED KERALA ROOF

Nethuni Sumanaweera

Above: Amphitheatre, 2023, Kerala, photograph by Syam Sreesylam.

What does it mean to build with others rather than for them? This question continues to shape the work of architect Vinu Daniel, whose practice, Wallmakers challenges the ideas of authorship, sustainability and the role of the architect. This article is a reflection on Inflection *co-editor Nethuni Sumanaweera's conversation with Vinu Daniel.*

Deep in Kerala, one of India's southernmost states, lies the Nisarga Art Hub. This is the creation of architect Vinu Daniel, for whom architecture is far more than just design. Since establishing Wallmakers in 2007, his studio has pursued a practice that is both experimental programmatically while utilising traditional techniques deeply embedded in its context. The result is an ever-evolving social, material and ecological collaboration drawn from local wisdom and environmental responsibility. This practice is sustained by human relationships that extend beyond the buildings themselves. In Daniel's view, joy and community are diffused throughout the architecture, it nurtures and sustains him.

The commission for the Nisarga Art Hub came from two musicians in search of a home and performance space overlooking the paddy fields of rural Kerala. Daniel wanted to create an expansive space for the pair, who were already holding classes for younger, upcoming musicians in the neighbourhood. This posed challenges, as the building not only needed to accommodate the family but also to make room for art practices and for the wider community's inclusion.

Important to the design was a vast, uninterrupted indoor volume for art and exchange. But one of the project's most iconic aspects has been the transformation of its sloped roof into a social platform. Despite its ambition, the couple felt that the Hub's internal space alone did not feel adequate and the creative utilisation of the roof emerged unexpectedly. The typical Kerala-style roof, instigated by a passing suggestion, gradually evolved into a key architectural gesture in the project. For Daniel, it became a means to explore not only the separation of interior and exterior spaces but also the intersection of domestic and collective experiences. The roof is a proposal for a reimagined amphitheatre for gathering and performance.

Once completed, the roof took on a life of its own. Visitors climbed it uninvited, filming drone videos and holding impromptu performances. The clients welcomed this spontaneous occupation. As a result, the building succeeded in becoming both a literal and symbolic place of congregation. This gesture lends itself to Daniel's broader belief that architecture cannot be divided from its community. Daniel, in fact, insists that no-one is separate from their community and his approach to architecture critiques the detachment characteristic of contemporary practice. Alongside such communal values, he has a reverence for both the land itself and the practices of its traditional owners. Both of these, he believes, are powerful teachers, which he utilises in his work.

Collective creation means that process and authorship are inseparable from use, an idea augmented by the project being a collaboration between Daniel and his wife, Oshin Varughese. In this way, the Nisarga Art Hub models itself on reciprocity and shared creativity. Love, labour and architecture are woven together, inseparable.

Material and Ethical Responsibility

Daniel's practice is led by a consistent commitment to material sustainability, informed by Gandhian principles. It follows the philosophy that the ideal house can be made from materials taken from the vicinity. For the Nisarga Art

Hub, this approach was enacted with intent and care. Roof tiles were crafted from neighbourhood discards, the mud walls formed from leftover laterite waste and construction debris and the flooring laid with the reclaimed wood of old logs. Almost 93% of the materials used were salvaged or repurposed. In this approach sustainability becomes a cultural and ethical practice. Rather than importing high-performance systems, Daniel draws from the immediate material landscape, a gesture that simultaneously reduces embodied energy and engages participation from the community at large. These measures are not regarded as a burden but rather as a responsibility and obligation.

Daniel cites Laurie Baker as an influence, with Baker viewing environmental consciousness as inseparable from social equity. By sourcing locally, reusing waste and engaging local labour, Daniel advocates for a democratic material culture that challenges the alienation of industrial construction.

Architecture Beyond Architects

Daniel offers a deeper challenge to the profession's place in society. He notes the rich history of people building together and claims that they will continue to do so with or without architects. Therefore, it is architects who risk obsolescence if they fail to understand the needs of humanity and of Earth.

Traditional ideas of the architect as an author should be reconsidered, Daniel asserts, with the architect's role instead framed as integrated. This role should be one of listening, adapting and working alongside others. He points to long-standing, collective systems of making as a source of inspiration and direction.

This critique extends to architectural education, which he says only encourages distance and hierarchy. He points to academic convention leading to both undue superiority and unhelpful constraint. In his view, the future of the profession lies in moving away from rigid boundaries separating architects from the people and places they hope to serve.

Reclaiming the Human in Architectural Practice

Daniel's reflections on architecture carry a quiet critique of the profession's modern lonesomeness. Too often, he observes, the work has shifted toward screens, software and managerial detachment. The result, he laments, is widespread unhappiness and he suggests that by reintroducing human connection into the making of buildings, we might rediscover a sense of joy in the profession.

Restraint

A clear expression of Daniel's design thinking comes in what he deliberately left undone at the Nisarga Art Hub. He believes that the building's greatest success lies in what didn't get built, noting a lack of furniture and the unbuilding of a part of the floor. This decision shows architecture as an act of restraint, one that invites flexibility over formal completion. By choosing absence, Daniel allows space for others to inhabit and reinterpret.

A Communal Architecture

The Nisarga Art Hub is a living extension of its community. The sloped roof, built from reclaimed tiles and inhabited by neighbours and musicians, has become a literal platform for gathering. It captures Daniel's belief that architecture's role is to encourage connection between people and landscape, between the past and the yet-to-come and between those who design and those who build.

At a time when architecture often leans toward spectacle, speed and technological flourish, Daniel's projects remind us that ecological design means taking social responsibility. This begins with empathy, with listening to the land and to those who live on it.

This is not simply the story of one building. It is a proposition for how we might practice differently. Only future generations, Daniel believes, will be able to judge his success.

Above: Stage, 2023, Kerala, photograph by Syam Sreesylam.

Above: Interior, 2023, Kerala, photograph by Syam Sreesylam.

LOVE & REPAIR

MUSICAL ARCHITECTURES OF SURVIVAL

Simona Castricum

I fell out of love with architecture in 2015. It became painfully clear it didn't reflect my values in practice, despite all its lofty aspirations. Its lexicon of delight and beauty didn't extend care into the studio door. It felt performative at best and was violent at worst. The love I was supposed to feel for architecture, a love I once believed in, started to feel like betrayal. So, I left.

I did not stop designing. I prioritised the architectures I imagined through music and transing. If architecture would not hold my body, I would create other spaces that did—into clubs, into lyrics, into songs.

I hate songs about nothing.
I hate architecture that insists upon neutrality even more.
I hate explaining my songs to people, yet here I am.

The last three records I've made, *Panic/Desire* (2020), *SINK* (2023) and my upcoming, unreleased album, with the working title *Love & Repair* (2026), have become the sites where I re-encounter architecture. Not through detailing car parks, but through embodiment, rupture and repair. These records are more than sonic projects; they are spatial practices. Architectures of growth. *Saturn Rules the Material World* (2023), the lone epitaphic offering by my project SaD with the late Daphne Camf, informs the trilogy sitting in its breach.

Panic/Desire was a transfeminist autoethnographic work. Writing, producing and performing it became a way of testing how music operates as architecture: mapping affect, risk and resistance through rhythm and resonance. In *Panic/Desire*, I name violence, how built environments inscribe normative gender, erase transness and uphold settler-colonial ideologies under the guise of neutrality. The album was written during a time of dislocation, as I sought to find my bodily autonomy and establish grounding research, to know my shit. To see the relationship between architecture and transphobia. This was the start of re-worlding: propositions of speculative places I could move through freely without being misgendered, policed, or made invisible. I wasn't designing buildings anymore. I was designing feeling.

I wrote *Panic/Desire* for community, to walk alongside my transgender siblings on the streets they've walked. To offer a language for what's long been known somatically and geographically, yet often unspoken. An explanation, as spatial recognition, a rendering of the affective architectures we design to survive. We strut at 120 bpm. To recognise the architectures we build through our awakenings and our archives, when no other space holds us. Jos Esteban Muñoz asks; "How do we stage utopia"? Not just a temporal phase, but a spatial one. *Panic/Desire* becomes that stage: a queer architecture of refusal, longing and becoming.[1]

The album, *Supertouch* was made for the trans club: that hyperreal site where performance serves survival, where what Dorian Corey describes as 'realness' becomes street armour, protection in the contested thresholds around the club. It is a space where beauty is political and proximity is complicated, because you're seen, but never enough, or too much.

Other songs on *Panic/Desire* wrestle with a different dissonance: the intimacy of virtual connection versus the ache of tactile distance. The song, 'The Half Light' recognises this emotional architecture to both protect and reveal, the threshold between stories, views and

**I hate songs about nothing.
I hate architecture that insists upon neutrality even more.
I hate explaining my songs to people—yet here I am.**

likes, where you're emotionally naked but physically vulnerable. If visibility without protection is a trap, then what keeps us safe? The song 'Panopticon' critiques the way we opt into surveillance for dopamine, exchanging privacy for proximity. 'The Present' is more direct, a resistance anthem, a line drawn against the daily violences of transmisogyny. In these neo-dark ages of Trumpian assaults on trans life, the times demand it. Five years on, these songs continue to evolve, not as fixed meanings, but as ongoing architectures of spatial and political interpretation, as well as dystopian predictions of civic life.

When the COVID-19 pandemic hit and Naarm entered lockdown in 2020, *Panic/Desire* took on an entirely new meaning. The record was no longer just about clubs, airports and streets—it became about solitude, longing and the architectures of the mind. What happens when all public space is withdrawn? What spaces do we create in our minds in times of social isolation? Who do we become when our bodies are seen only in the digital? The album morphed into virtual architecture, a place for queer longing to shapeshift and survive. Despite potentiality, Muñoz's horizon felt like a tomorrow that would never come.[3]

And then came the album *SINK*. As we slowly emerged from our five-kilometre radius, from solitude and intimate partner bubbles, the world didn't get easier, it grew heavier, more fragile, immune-compromised. The album asks: What happens when the mind turns inward and starts to attack itself? What remains when desire collapses, when connection disintegrates, when loss becomes unspoken and death is total? What's left are ghosts. An infinite smallness becomes frontier psychology.

I had given up on surface resistance and let myself drop. *SINK* is about submergence, about going under, surrender, dissolving, addiction. It reflects spatial refusal: what if I don't want to be seen? What if I close my eyes and flatline in the corner? What if the very idea of visibility, of transparency, openness, access, is part of the architecture that harms me? The party became a different kind of studio; it became unsafe. Darkness and ketamine became the materials, "in a hole that I searched for an answer exposed me for all of my weakness."

SINK was written inside grief, not around it. It doesn't resolve. It doesn't offer escape, as much as it tries to. Instead, it lingers above our heads in suspended animation. In the detuned portamento, the unstable formant modulations of *Whomst?* speak to affective conditions that make architectures of love impossible. Sonically and emotionally, the record became a form of spatial mourning. The absence of physical space was a provocation: if I can't occupy the world as I am, then I will haunt it. I will build space from memory, sadness, motion with arpeggiators and percussion. I will perform my trauma on my terms; stadium techno reimagined as an intimate relationship.

In this zone, I think about what Ellen van Neerven writes in *Throat* of love as 'haunting.' A spectral, aggrieved love. The kind that pulses through grief and survival. "We're not supposed to know what people really think of us until we're dead."[4] It is a line that hovers like a ghost itself. That 'after-ness,' deferred recognition, or delayed tenderness makes sense to me. This is the space where *Love & Repair* begins to take shape, not as healing, but as lingering. Not recovery but maintenance. Where *Panic/Desire* forged queer architectures under constraint and SINK spiralled through the spaces grief creates, *Love & Repair* opens into what becomes possible in the worlds we build.

The album, *Saturn Rules the Material World* offered a moment of emergence, of grasping at something, barely, amid heartbreak. I wrote it for my late bandmate and close friend: "I burnt the soles of my feet running out of those halls of defeat." That line still burns. Daphne reminds me: "In my radical self-acceptance, I'm grateful for the heartache." Love is the teacher, nuggets, gifts of wisdom.

Love & Repair opens into what becomes possible in the worlds we build next. Here, love is neither romantic nor redemptive. Love is labour. Love is scaffolding. Love is maintenance. Love is forgiveness. Imperfect, provisional and always asking: what are we even repairing when the structure was hostile from the start?

The Dolls Know, like its predecessor *The Present*, is an urgent refusal. It stands at the edge of performativity and says: fuck you. "Harm disguised by broken dreams, ambush camouflage in ally schemes." We've seen it all before. The instrumental is relentless, vocals unflinching. "I did the bags, I did the pills, but still the transmisogyny kills, 'cos the dolls know." Protect the dolls, my ass. We keep us safe.

'Spiritual' is a soft architecture, not of walls but of breath and kindness. It is a self-built sanctuary, a whisper of reprieve from the noise. "Just for today, I will be something kinder to my heart so I can breathe." It is a rendering, not of buildings or some churchy spirituality but an image of surviving another day in a world that keeps demanding your eradication; "the parts they never let me show, I call them home." In *All About Love*, bell hooks writes of spirituality not as belief, but as practice, a soulful experience rooted in self-love and care, extending outward into community.[5] It is this vision that *Spiritual* gestures toward: a mode of living where love is action, not sentiment; where softness is not weakness but resistance; where tending to oneself is a precondition for solidarity.

'Sweet Relief' expresses the exhaustion of yearning. It asks: "If love is worth all of this paying for, I don't know what I'm trying to save it for." In architecture, we call this questioning retrofitting, trying to make a situationship functional within a structure that was never built for you in the first place. Living in orbit to the relentless assemblage of the cisgender paradigm, that fatigue of resistance is foundational to trans spatial production. Still, we make do, carving out utopias in the liminal, repurposing the ruins into something that might hold us until it doesn't.

Lyrics don't fix anything; they reveal what's been left unsaid. That work of naming the unspoken, the unbelievable truth, of giving form to affect, is a kind of design. A kind of love. Like abolition. Like Free Palestine. Love is an action. It's not a T-shirt. It's something we do. *Love & Repair* is a kind of elegy for all the things we tried to hold together.

All the ways we failed each other. It doesn't promise healing, it holds the grief, the multiple truths of knowing we may not ever get there. "What keeps us side by side is how we've come to love and repair." It is a methodology, a way of staying close, even through failure.
This music resists beauty in the Vitruvian sense, it's about care. Not aesthetics, but ethics. Not form, but feeling. Its architecture defies temporalities but is built to bear witness—a record of what we tried, who we held, what broke us open and what lies ahead after an ideation of oblivion, beyond suffering.

Love & Repair does not offer grand visions. It asks of us a new set of smaller, honest questions: Can a performance be a shelter? Can silence be structure? Can a song hold us spatially when the world will not? In the same way I became suspicious of architecture as inherently benevolent, *Love & Repair* interrogates the role music plays in love's myth-making. While all of us, especially trans lives, are deserving of love, none of us are entitled to it. Yet popular music often insists otherwise: that heartbreak is betrayal, that desire demands reciprocation, that love is owed, *after all I've done for you!* I wanted to write against the weaponisation of love. Rather, to be intentional, to be spatial, about longing without expectation. To sing not from possession, but from release. Heartbreak not as failure, but as a place to build from—a kind of power.

Dean Spade suggests in *Love in a F*cked-Up World*: to access liberation, we can unlearn the romance myths we've inherited. That means becoming actively curious about how we've been shaped by normativity and love, by culture, by politics and by the archives of family, partners, (dis)connection, longing and of place.[6] I use 'archives' here in the epistemological sense drawn from Ann Cvetkovich's queer approach to trauma, where memory, affect and embodiment function as counter-archives to dominant cultural narratives. This framing resists heteronormative logics of linear family structures or romantic resolution, instead opening space for queer and trans modalities of feeling and knowing. In this way, music and architecture are hybrid disciplines. They are deeply intertwined ways of designing survival through creative practice. While forces like archives, partnerships, community, bodies and trauma shape us in ways we can't always control, the acts of rupture, repair and accountability create openings. They hold the possibility of joy, not through permanence but by insisting on presence.

Graffiti by a Vis beach in Komi a, "Love is bull shit, there is no happy end." A takeaway from my summer EU holiday. At 50, it rings true, or maybe that's a Cure-esque myth I've inherited from *Disintegration*. I see myself reflected in that dichotomous urban gesture of nihilism and love. They know.

Still, despite everything, I keep choosing love, designing from it, writing through it, searching for it, frightened by it. For better or worse, perhaps it is still the first and only radical act left.

Above: Unknown artist, Love is bull shit, there is no happy end, 2025, Komiža, photograph by Simona Castricum.

01 Muñoz, J. E. (2009). *Cruising Utopia: The Then and There of Queer Futurity.* New York: New York University Press, 99.

02 Livingston, J. (Producer). (1992). *Paris Is Burning* [Film]. USA: Mirimax.

03 Muñoz, J. E. (2009). *Cruising Utopia: The Then and There of Queer Futurity*. New York: New York University Press, 24.

04 van Neerven, E. (2020) *Throat*. St Lucia, QLD: University of Queensland Press, 4.

05 hooks, b. (2000). *All About Love: New Visions.* William Morrow. New York.), 13.

06 Spade, D. (2025). *Love In a F*cked-Up World: How to Build Relationships Hook Up and Raise Hell together*. Algonquin Books of Chapel Hill. New York, 97.

07 Cvetkovich, A. (2003). *An Archive of Feelings: Trauma, Sexuality, and Lesbian Public Cultures.* Duke University Press, 8.

THREE MORE LOVE LETTERS

Jimenez Lai (Bureau Spectacular)

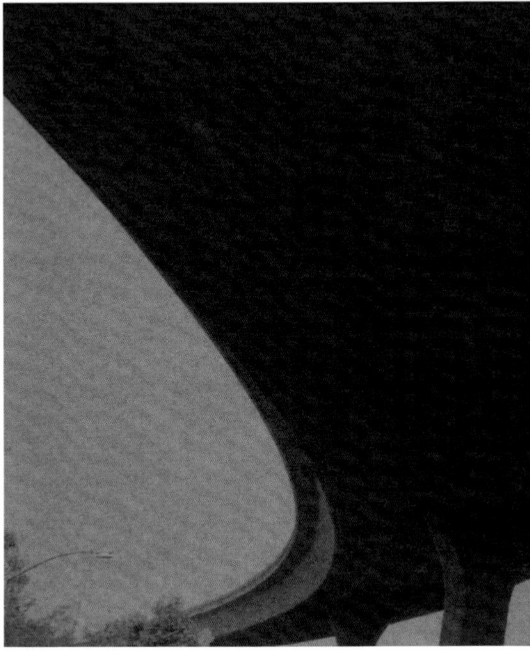

Nearly a decade ago I wrote a series of ten love letters professing my admiration towards a range of buildings, publications, or ideas, that affected me deeply.[1] Time has passed and I am producing an addendum to that series of thoughts. Robert Venturi once said: "You don't have to like something to learn from it." In this vein, these new love letters discuss projects I may, or may not, have loved at first sight. Eventually however, I found myself compelled by all three in one way or another.

On Infrastructure

The new LACMA building by Peter Zumthor and SOM asks a question about the aesthetics of infrastructure.

In Los Angeles, infrastructure is a matter of sensation. The first thing this Zumthor building reminded me of was not another museum, but Catherine Opie's *Freeways*. You do not visit it, or pause within it—instead, you circulate through it. Opie's photos capture the spirit of Los Angeles, because the vehicular infrastructure in this city is the defining landscape. The monuments are the things that people use every day: the 10s, 5s, 405s, 101s. In Europe, perhaps the lingering impact of *Reyner Banham Loves Los Angeles* persists—maybe from Zumthor's perspective, in LA, it is contextual to be infrastructural.

Zumthor's solution to an LA detail is none. No 'Zumthor' tectonics, no tactile joinery, no expression of connection system. Just exposed concrete and curtain wall, relying on the lack of resolution of an infrastructural scale. The rawness is palpable—but maybe that is what it means to evoke a contemporary form of the 'sublime.' It is why Ando is compelling to some and why Zumthor's bath remains the ultimate sensorial manifestation of an architecture of poetry and shadows.

Its lack of detail is reminiscent of another project, also not a building, but Paul Virilio's publication, *Bunker*

Above: Catherine Opie, Untitled #1, 1994, Platinum Print, 5.7x17.1 cm, image courtesy of Regen Projects and Catherine Opie.

Archeology. Here, masses are shaped by warfare, perception and paranoia. Instead of defense, it is display; instead of a coastline, it is Wilshire Boulevard. The building feels like an artifact from a future past, a 'suspended ruin' of the war zones of the Anthropocene. I could not help but wonder: if a future archaeologist were to unearth this, alongside Ice Age mammals preserved in tar pits, would they appear to have been part of the same extinction event? But from the edges, there appears something else: a new vantage point of Wilshire Boulevard. A view that makes me think not of history, but of Ed Ruscha's *Every Building on the Sunset Strip* (1966). You are no longer a pedestrian or a driver here. You are floating—an observer on a band of culture, surfing the city on a concrete wafer.

This building is confident; perhaps a little unresolved. Sublime means you will have to overthink. Just feel it. But maybe that is precisely the point. It does not explain itself, it just is. An infrastructural tarte flambe on a boulevard of mammoths.

On Typology

In revisiting the Los Angeles Cathedral of Our Lady of the Angels by Spanish architect Rafael Moneo, I am reminded of how Moneo broke the cross.

In twenty-first century Los Angeles, a church is a metaphysical machine at the speed of cars. In each case, the notion of a contemporary religious typology undergoes transformations. Unlike its European predecessors, Our Lady of the Angels is surrounded by cars—not just passing by on local speed limits, but the full velocity of the 101 Freeway. This is more than a site condition; it is a cultural idiosyncrasy of Los Angeles.

Historically, the cruciform of the cathedral was not only in the plan to organise the buildings; it also performed a

Above: Rafael Moneo, Cathedral of Our Lady of the Angels, 1996-2002, Los Angeles, photograph by Michael Moran.

political function, urbanistically. Take Siena, for example. There, the Duomo occupies the top of an incline, where the nave aligns with citizens on foot. Urbanistically, the speed of the space in front of the cathedral becomes a matter of civic infrastructure: gatherings of slow conversations, debates, or other informal encounters take place here, with the facade of the church in the backdrop to mark the occasion. Cathedrals are not solely religious buildings. They punctuate civic life and act as a backdrop for public discourse.

By dislocating the cruciform plan, Moneo reroutes the procession away from the expected front towards a bent entry sequence. Sacrilegious? No; rather, a high-wire typological risk in response to the infrastructural grammars of a high-speed city. Along its Grand Avenue elevation is where one would anticipate to find the cathedral's primary entry—but this is not the case. Instead, the journey begins behind the apse, along a meandering path far from the logic of a similar typology. This dislocation is not just functional, nor merely symbolic. It is a contextual move that says that the speed of Los Angeles has deformed the cross. A piazza above the apse is now the pedestrian cove, complete with access to parking and pay meters. Driving along the 101 is in itself another experience—because at that speed, the cathedral becomes a billboard.

Whereas the traditional cathedral ceiling may include vaults and domes—or, cylinders and spheres that could perform acoustically (before modern audio systems)—the ceiling panels of Our Lady of the Angels conceals a gap

Above: Rafael Moneo, Cathedral of Our Lady of the Angels, 1996-2002, Los Angeles, photograph by Michael Moran.

stuffed with equipment. No frescoed heavens populated by saints and angels; Moneo's flat ceiling is a technical field, a muted coffered volume concealing a vast array of acoustic, audiovisual, theatrical and mechanical systems. One might recall the Wyly Theater by OMA and REX—a building in which the mechanics of stagecraft are rendered architectural. But where the Wyly externalises its superfly, Moneo internalises it. This ceiling questions typology today. Here, the cathedral is a hybridised vessel of assembly and performance, where the spiritual is inseparable from the technical and the theatrical.

At Our Lady of the Angels, in place of stained-glass windows one finds thinly cut alabaster, backlit by daylight. Where the medieval cathedral used stained glass to communicate the bible—telling stories to a mostly illiterate public through luminous graphic narratives—Moneo offers an abstraction where the saints, annunciations and gospel icons dissolve into cosmic patterns. In our current, mostly literate era, the bible does not need to be illustrated. However, in the alabaster, another secret of the universe is on display. Through the swirls and patterns of marbled material, an unreadable story is yet again in front of us. Its patterns recall neither heaven nor earth, but something in between: the natural flows of space dust, the slow-moving galactic specks of nebulae, the mysterious realms beyond the Hubble Telescope. These walls do not teach us about God; instead, they return us to our inability to comprehend. Nature is presented as a site of metaphysical unknowables. Two decades later, this remains one of my favourite buildings in Los Angeles. Perhaps this building is overlooked because religious architecture no longer anchors contemporary discourse. But Our Lady of the Angels deserves renewed attention—not as an icon, but as a typological recalibration. Here, Moneo reopens the question of what it means to be sacred in a modern metropolis—where faith must navigate with speed, technology and knowledge.

On Tautness

Diagrammatically, Kukje Gallery by SO-IL is a dumpling.

In 2010, SO-IL won the MoMA PS1 competition with their project *Pole Dance*. *Pole Dance* was a movable, flexible and interactive structural system. Its network of poles with rotary joints pushed onto the draping net above with a reverse-tufting effect that allowed the tips of the columns to compressively push against the tensile surface and create hyperbolic paraboloids.

The Kukje Gallery was realised in 2012. Lessons learned from *Pole Dance* were evident here, in three-dimensions, where tautness was transposed volumetrically. The cantilevering concrete components of the building reflected the interior organisations and programmatic distributions that jutted out of the primary volume, but these protrusive masses stretched the wrapping mesh to create a tight-fitted dumpling. Every protrusion, every drip of architectural support underneath was rendered legible through this chainmail skin. SO-IL's envelope was not about concealment, but about conductivity. Light passes; air passes; perception wavers. Such translucent architecture seduces us through the many almosts: almost solid, almost private, almost revealed.

Around this time, SO-IL also embarked on a collaboration with artist Ana Prvacki. Ana Prvacki's 2007 performance piece, *Tent, Quartet, Bows and Elbows,* featured a quartet performing a song inside of a translucent tent where the movements of the musicians were captured onto the bumping, bulging and protruding through the bows and elbows. Was this art piece also a dumpling? A live one, yes. In some ways, this performance piece was an active and animated version of the Kukje Gallery diagram—but instead of musicians, it was the choreographed circulation paths of the gallery visitors. In 2017, the team created *l'air pour l'air*: a performance piece that allowed the artist and the architects' shared thesis to converge.

Wrapped Reichstag (1985) by Christo and Jeanne-Claude demonstrates a different type of wrapping. A nearly seamless and abstracted replica of the building underneath, this cloak is almost a custom-fit bespoke outfit for the content within. Whereas SO-IL worked on tight-fitting dumplings, Christo and Jeanne-Claude produced well-fitting, nearly perfect jackets for architecture. The work of Jorge Otero-Pailos also features perfect-fit wraps. His project, *The Ethics of Dust Series*, casts existing walls or facades using latex. By pulling the detailed features off, exact replicas are perfectly documented onto a thin sheet, verbatim. It is as though the tailoring is a high-resolution reproduction of the existing content.

In Joshua Prince Ramus' 2006 Ted Talk, he discussed the design process of the Seattle Public Library: a hyper-rationalised shifting of programs, enclosed in a tight-fitting that wraps around the floating masses. As a predecessor to the Kukje Gallery, the Seattle Public Library was a low-resolution version of a dumpling. At a much larger scale, the outline of the Seattle Public Library is rationalised as a set of straight lines for a higher constructibility. At Kukje, hyper rationalism has developed into a translucent dumpling: program begets form, but when wrapped with soft, translucent chain mail, diagram is a dumpling.

As the love letters have grown, so has my passion for architecture. In a world where the measure of success is rarely about the quality of architecture, I use these letters to decipher why I continue to love it.

01 See Jimenez Lai, "Ten Love Letters," in *Perspecta* 52: Ensemble, ed. Charlotte Algie and Alicia Pozniak (Cambridge, MA: MIT Press, 2019), 278-287.

Above: SO-IL, Pole Dance, 2010, MoMA, New York, photograph by Iwan Baan.
Below: SO-IL, Kukje Gallery, 2012, Seoul, photograph by Iwan Baan.

LOVE AND THE CENTRAL GOLDFIELDS ART GALLERY

IN CONVERSATION WITH NERVEGNA REED ARCHITECTURE

Anna Nervegna & Toby Reed

Above: A displaced geometry replaces a column and a wall to prevent falls from the ramp, Central Goldfields Art Gallery, 2022, photograph by John Gollings.

How can the concept of love, in all of its complexity and ambiguity, inform architectural practice and engage with community? Inflection *co-editors Sunny Brearley and Charlotte Schaller sat down with Anna Nervegna and Toby Reed to discuss the Central Goldfields Gallery on Dja Dja Wurrung Country in Central Victoria.*

Could you speak about what the process of engaging with Country and community looks like in real practice?

AN: We felt like carers of this process. Engaging with Country is a process of deep attention and consideration, of seeing from new perspectives and acknowledging the long history of denial and rewriting of Indigenous culture by the colonial culture. As architects, we must recognise this intricacy and explore how ideas of Country can shape our understanding of sculpting space, site and program. In a way, this becomes an act of caring, caring for place, for histories and for the relationships that define them.

At the Central Goldfields Art Gallery, our approach moved beyond a singular architectural vision towards one of shared agency, acknowledging the Dja Dja Wurrung culture alongside the colonial history of the site in this goldrush town. From the outset, we felt a responsibility to consider the multifaceted whole rather than to impose a fixed idea. The design process itself became a focus of listening, understanding and exploring how notions of Country may be allowed to filter through the project. The process became generative, allowing a deeper spatial and cultural response to emerge, one that reflected how Country could quietly and meaningfully shape the architecture.

In terms of the existing building(s), the project began with a modest request: to install an accessible ramp into the main gallery for the community. We soon recognised that this change would remove a key display wall and disrupt the original proportions of the former fire station. The limited budget fostered a heightened sense of attention, for both the building's heritage, user groups and the community it serves.

TR: We felt a responsibility, yet as architects, how could we handle this complex idea? How do we merge this with the very complex history of what colonisation did to another culture, attempted erasure but still existing now and vibrant. There are many ways of endeavouring to apply an Indigenous exploration of Country to architecture. Often, what we see by architects is very literal, iconic images on the building or on the carpet. But since it is an art gallery, we wanted to find a deeper way of connecting with Country and we wanted to explore and critique the notion of the white cube for the artists and the artworks, while recognising reconciliation in the spaces.

Right: Section through the entry foyer showing the triangular skylight inserted into the ceiling, allowing cinematic views of the Fire Tower from inside the building, drawing by Nervegna Reed Architects.

Opposite above: View through the triangular skylight, Central Goldfields Art Gallery, 2022, photograph by John Gollings.

Opposite below: View of the split circle wall from the gallery's permanent collection space, Central Goldfields Art Gallery, 2022, photograph by John Gollings.

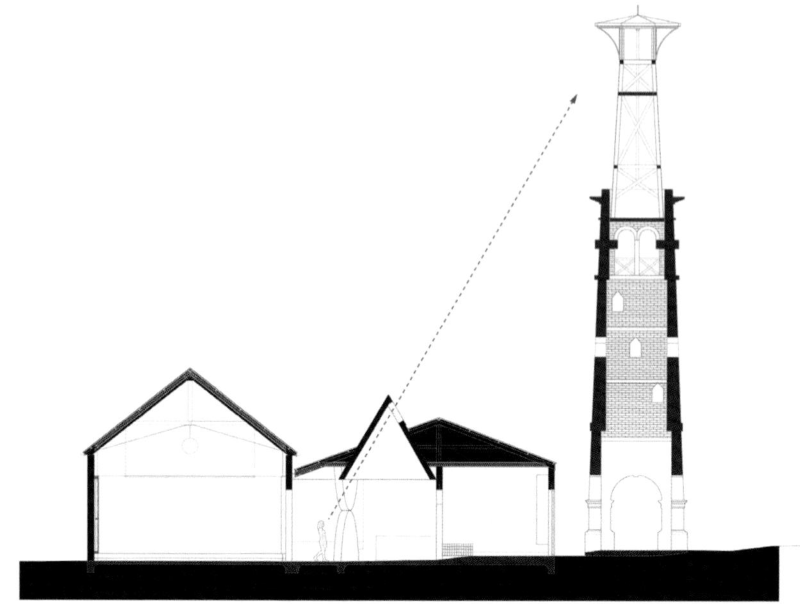

Now that Central Goldfields has been built and running for a while, how has it been received? Is the Dja Dja Wurrung community pleased with the garden and do they feel like it has been a successful integration of both histories?

TR: Definitely. I think everyone is very proud of it. The council wanted a public building that helped reconciliation and it has now become a place for all people in the community to meet.

AN: In a small town like Maryborough, the gallery has become a true gathering place; whenever there's an opening, the whole community comes together. It goes beyond the program and establishes a place for connection. The project ultimately created a far greater and more meaningful experience than we had anticipated. Some of the elements include the revitalisation of the former fire station and bell tower, together with the introduction of the Indigenous Garden, which were intended to draw new audiences into the gallery to view art and elements of the native garden for all members of the community.

You have previously spoken about 'surgically cutting' into this nineteenth century building, itself an anti-architectural, anti-colonial act, while capturing the view of the colonial tower. Why was that important?

TR: When we met with Dja Dja Wurrung Elders and Djaara members in the Wartaka (a coming together with purpose), they all loved the tower. They wanted to celebrate it and not see it as only a symbol of oppression. They were saying, "Yes, it's a beautiful tower. We've got to celebrate it." By then we had already begun cutting views to the tower and to the proposed Indigenous Garden. Each cut was itself an anti-colonial, anti Victorian manoeuvre as it went against the logic of Victorian architectural composition. The Victorians would not have thought to do this and that's the shock of it. The cuts bring the outside inside, captured in a frame and create a very cinematic feel as you move through the space, not within the Victorian tradition. If this renovation had been carried out 35 years ago, the architect would likely have attempted to bring the building back exactly to its 1891 state, which would have reinforced the Victorian ideology. We attempted to 'cut' into the building surgically to find other realities.

AN: We were aware of the different boundaries of the project, the fine line between respecting the history of the fire station and bell tower and wanting to respect the Indigenous culture that was dominated by it. This awareness of the tension between the two created a dual attitude and sensitive response. Artists' processes such as Gordon Matta-Clark, who would surgically erase things and cut holes, made us think that this could be a process which does not have to be about embellishing and inserting, but rather a process of removing and revealing.

When considering how to acknowledge both histories, we thought of Marcia Langton's notion of 'intwined histories,' which examines the complex and often fraught relationships between Indigenous Australians and broader Australian society, both colonial and post-colonial. We cannot deny or separate these histories, nor absolve ourselves of their legacy. The intention, therefore, was to interweave them spatially, allowing architecture to act as a gesture of connection and maybe reconciliation, a reframing which oscillates as we walk through the gallery.

Colonial buildings are traditionally introspective and closed, yet our intervention created new ways of seeing, framing the tower, revealing its quiet beauty from within and opening views toward the Indigenous Garden. Even if visitors are not consciously aware of this interweaving, the spatial vistas offer moments with native vegetation and water, Country and the interior coexist. It is an experience meant to be felt intuitively, a dialogue between the artwork, the building, the tower and the Dja Dja Wurrung landscape.

You call it 'displaced geometry,' it is present in this project and in other projects. What is it? Is this a return to basic principles?

TR: Our architectural manoeuvres, geometric or otherwise, are often about creating intentional disjuncture within the ordinary. The idea is to intervene in the everyday. Many architectural projects are needed to be ordinary, yet sometimes we need a shock to jolt us from it, to make us think and see our place in reality. It functions much like one of Duchamp's ready-mades, to take an everyday object, put it in the wrong place, or do something unexpected to it and it changes our thought process. Through that displacement you become aware of your reality, or of the building you are standing in.

When we first arrived at the site, the building had been so messed up by terrible additions over time that our instinct was to get rid of everything that had been added, erasure as design technique. We thought of Rauschenberg rubbing out the de Kooning drawing (1953). We thought it could be a great way to design; that is, to design with an eraser rather than the pencil. When you walk through the gallery now, the things we uncovered felt like erasures: we found footprints in the old concrete, like ghosts of past actions and any walls we pulled down we filled with a different-coloured concrete.

The council wanted a dialogue of reconciliation between the gallery and the Indigenous Garden, but this was not explicitly in the brief as no one knows exactly how to achieve it. We needed a response that was not the average Victorian style, but one that, at first jolts, then deepens understanding (like love does). To complete the Victorian architecture as originally intended, would have excluded the Indigenous Garden and those histories. Instead, we restored the building against that ideology, with the aim to jolt, whether

Above: View of the main gallery façade with glass sliding door set behind the old fire station doors, Central Goldfields Art Gallery, 2022, photographs by John Gollings.

Right: Plan showing the spaces that have been cut through the building fabric to the Indigenous Garden to the north and the tower above.

1 Town Hall link
2 Main gallery
3 Pop-up gallery
4 Loading area
5 Education room
6 Collection store
7 Administration
8 Permanent collection
9 Reception
10 Skylight to tower
11 Sculpture

Left: Street view of the Indigenous Garden, the tower and the 'moon wall' to the education room which glows in the garden at dusk, Central Goldfields Art Gallery, 2022, photograph by Toby Reed.
Right: Interior view of the 'moon wall', Central Goldfields Art Gallery, 2022, photograph by John Gollings.

cognitively or experientially, to make us aware that multiple histories can work in a space. In these situations, you must be very careful when designing as ideas considered progressive now may change meaning over time. That's why we worked with abstraction and space objects rather than iconography.

AN: The idea of 'displaced geometry' became an important concept to us, a way of becoming conscious not only of form but of how geometries and spatial ideas travel between art forms, cultures and histories.
As a parallel architectural gesture, we introduced a circular 'moon' wall in the education room facing the garden, a spatial echo of the garden and a place for gathering and reflection, described by the Elders as a kind of talking / meeting circle. Also, through the *Wartaka*, the Elders identified shared themes between the former fire station and Indigenous culture, particularly the elements of fire and water. These became guiding ideas for the *Garingilang Gatjin Wii*, the garden of Fire and Water.

In offering a displaced geometry we also recognise what is shared, a way to establish a connection, not only between the garden and the building but between the two cultures and histories. It is through this connection that the project seeks to explore, in a small way, to healing Country.

In recent years, have you noticed some change in architects' ethical responsibilities toward the physical environment? More generally, is the profession changing its approach at all—and why does it remain so challenging for universities to teach this?

AN: Yes, the profession is always evolving over time and in terms of presenting an Indigenous or First Nations culture (whether it is in a curriculum or in the practice), we cannot simply respond in obvious European way. When looking at First Nation culture on a deeper level, it is very much about broader notions of nonlinear time and higher concepts rather than decorative elements and patterns.

TR: There has been a big change. While many people are unsure about how to respond, some rely on token talk, sure, but dialogue is good, nonetheless. The conversation and collaboration about these issues and services is really important and is very different from past architectural dialogue. In architecture there is no single clear method to achieve ideas in space and form, it is always slightly ambiguous and open to multiple interpretations. This is the beauty of architecture as a discipline, but it's very hard or impossible, to teach an absolute method.

Whether Country or something else, you can attempt to put ideas into a building, but whether they are 'there' is uncertain. As Derrida said about writing, authorial intent matters less than how it is experienced. We often experience things in buildings that were not originally intended. There is possibly no prescribed way to incorporate Country. We can attempt to do this but you cannot be certain you are achieving it. Ultimately what matters is dialogue during the process and the finished work and how people engage with it, in the multiple different interpretations. So, we put forward prompts like displaced geometries, such as cutting a circle in half and set one half in the 'wrong' place because a column had to go there. We propose things that might trigger ideas, but we do not know exactly how they will be read.

Do you ever find yourselves revisiting the same precedent over time, especially those you explored at university? How have these formative ideas and the architectural language you have developed continued to influence your current practice?

AN: Our engagement with architecture is inherently exploratory, rooted in creative processes and diverse theoretical approaches. We all revisit things (not just precedents) and find them reoccurring in projects. We have always had a deep connection for art and culture and we are driven by a curiosity about space and form and where architecture may intersect with other disciplines; exploring the boundaries of what architecture can be.

TR: We do find that there is a consistency between what we did as students and what we are doing now, that elements and ideas keep reoccurring. Sometimes you go on a design tangent and you realise later that it might be wrong or right, you just don't know at first. But there is a consistency that comes out over time which is unintentional.

We do not often link love with architecture—it's an emotion, but the more you think about it, the more you realise how connected the two are. Is love in architecture still important or has its significance changed?

TR: I was thinking about cinema and cinematic genre in this context, like the range from the ordinary to the *L'Amour fou* of surrealism, or the suburban romcom versus the extreme (for instance) 'couple on the run' sub-genre, like *Gun Crazy* (1950) or *Bonnie and Clyde* (1967). It's a useful cinematic way to describe a whole range of ideas about love: the boring, the everyday, the clich and the extreme or irrational. Architecture spans that range too. These elements all need each other in a city to work. All buildings cannot be the same, just one of these types of love, or the city becomes a monotonous prison.

AN: Emotion and architecture are intrinsically linked. People have an emotional response to their built environment. Beyond the delivery of a brief there has to be more and we are wired for impact whether it is traditional or not. I think architects are very generous; as Jacques Lacan said, love is giving what you don't have to someone who doesn't exist. Love versus desire.

TR: As architects, you need a passion or love for society, culture as well as for chance or the accident, sometimes things can happen on site or with clients which are unexpected and stressful.

You need the patience that it will resolve itself. But in any relationship, you have to juggle everything and still keep sight of the goal or the passion for the project. As a profession architecture is creative, but high risk and often lowly paid. Anyone running or working in a small company takes on a high risk compared to the return. So, there is an aspect of love for humanity or community working in most architects because of this. You can also look at the Le Corbusier model of the architect as a kind of monk or priest, serving a society out of love and trying to improve society and make everyone happier, even if misguided.

Love (as a concept) is possibly about either becoming the other, or becoming immersed with the 'other' that leads to a deeper understanding. And so architectural space or form, as alien 'other' that we become acquainted with, immersed in, can offer new experiences outside of the everyday and present a deeper understanding of space, yourself or the world.

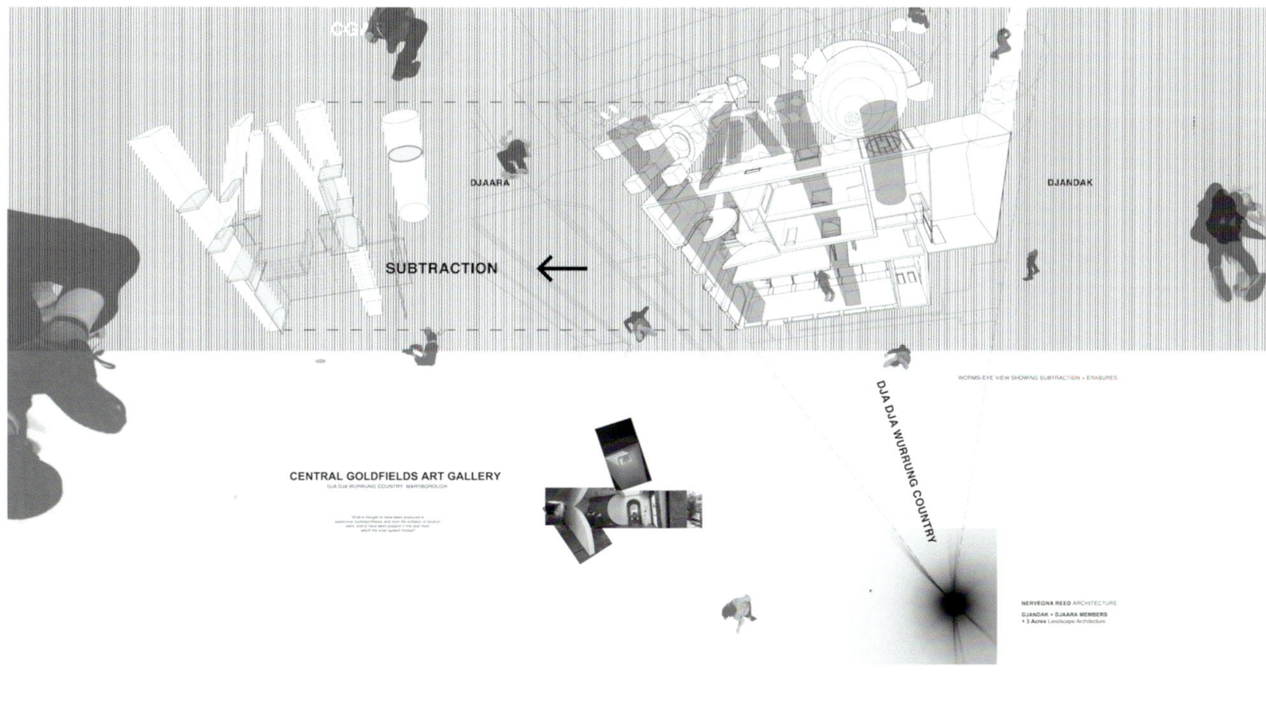

Above: Interior of Gallery, Central Goldfields Art Gallery, 2022, photograph by John Gollings.
Below: Spatial diagram for the 2023 Venice Biennale Australian Pavilion showing the process of subtraction used to create space objects which connect the interior with the Indigenous Garden tower, drawing by Nervegna Reed Architects.

LOVEWARE

Samiha Meem

Right: Samiha Meem, Ava and Nathan, 2025.
Left: Samiha Meem, the IBM System 360, 1964.

The search for "love" in my inbox returns not confessions or vows, but automated dispatches from Wealthsimple, SSENSE and Angelika Film Center. Maybe what I'm chasing is scattered across these fragments—or perhaps it comes later, once financial security, raw denim and indie thriller tickets have managed to impress a fledgling crush. Once, however, love was peripheral to daily affairs—if not a direct threat to church and state-sanctioned marriage, monogamy and reproduction. All its passion, though made ubiquitous by poets, philosophers, religious intelligentsia, industrialists and physicians, remained underwritten as a non-utilitarian expenditure: tempered, always to be left untouched. The secular reform of such half-choked desire into the modern bind of freedom and choice marked an unprecedented expansion of its public resonance, naturalising love as the dominant cultural apparatus through which we accept submission. Our economic and emotional temperaments were drawn into each other irreversibly to make up a unified regime of privatised feeling, brutal decisionisms and bluff satisfactions. This greased the expansion of capitalism to, inevitably, deliver the frictionless swipes of a billion-dollar techno-industrial love complex, where the promise of love acculturated the rhythm of an insatiable appetite so that a finite world of infinite consumables could be held upright. The left-brained, sorting through specialty appeals, financial liabilities, ideological misalignments, bad habits and bad hairlines from an endless stack of already-sanitised possibilities, meets an improbable optimism that some inviolate passion, if it ever were, could yet appear. In a cold reversal, we must grasp at love even as we stumble around in the dark.

It is understandable, then, that the participants of the U.S. Netflix reality series *Love Is Blind* surrender to another blind setup of depth-by-force. Each season relocates to a new city and cuts a cross-section of resident heterosexuals: marriage-minded, allegedly, but trapped in the superficial stutter of dating technologies. Singles arrive at the 68,000-square-foot California soundstage, where they are cloistered in pods to date within an unseen pool based solely on "who they are on the inside," (though already pre-screened for age, occupation, psychological stability, baseline attractiveness and an ineffable X-factor casting directors call a "good citizen").[2] After ten days, contestants enter provisional engagements. Man and woman are brought together in a ceremonial unveiling, before being routed through 'real world' compressions—honeymoon hotels, cohabitation condos, family visits and after-work happy hours—to decide, at the altar a month later, whether to marry or walk away.

This self-described 'experiment' opposes clinical conventions of modern dating and exhorts more enchanted forms of romance. It recalls Lee Mackinnon's distinction between literary and computational "discourse machines" of love. The literary—idealised in novels, frescoes and symphonies as 'true' romance—is contingent on codes of conduct imbued with meaning by religious, scientific, political, or economic forces, repeated so often they appear as natural emotional and libidinal reflexes. These codes are calculated twice: once to produce the effect of love and again to erase evidence of effort.[3] The enchantment must appear recovered yet reinforced as inseparable from technical arrangement.

The computational accelerates this probabilistic function through "technologies of choice," which, as Eva Illouz notes, engineers mechanisms by which we reach seemingly autonomous conclusions.[4] Rather than delivering a more robust version of security premised by the unidirectional literary machine, the computational traffics an indeterminate pursuit of love and exposes the limits of such hypercognised calculation.[5] The narration of the show follows the literary order, yet the pods—the environmental apparatus through which this unfolds—are enhanced with spatio-technical systems drawn from the computational: signal modulation, logistical protocols, bounded subjectivities and prosthetic interfaces. Their tight-range simulation establishes stable terms for indexing how the built environment participates in these discourses, which frame love as both given to and received from the machine and—indelibly—of the machine itself.

Cool Transmissions

The dates take place in soundproofed hexagonal pods, designed from blueprints the production company and designer developed as integral to their pitch to Netflix.[6] The 30 pods form a two-by-fifteen layout that bisects the soundstage into male and female territories, including separate halls and lounges, with the singles facing toward one another to speak through an opaque LED wall on the central axis. As the title suggests, this bipartite prophylactic environment aims to eliminate physical impressions so that participants can more efficiently 'find connection.' It calls to mind the computational *techne* of communicating love naturalised in the public imagination by Charles and Ray Eames for IBM through their 1953 film *A Communication Primer* which introduced information theories to architects. *Primer* shuffles through disparate images of everyday life until settling into discernible patterns made legible through cross-fades, rhythmic pacing and minute visual similarities. Its climax splices familiar symbols of love—cartoon hearts, human mouths, The Birth of Venus—with sender-channel-receiver diagrams from Claude E. Shannon's 1948 seminal communication theory. The diagram shows communication as a linear chain: source, destination and a channel vulnerable to "noise" that interferes with the message space. To temper this channel, language is read as having a statistical pattern that, by separating form from meaning, could make transmission more efficient and predictable. More noise meant more 'information' available for calculation.

Primer argues that "I love you," in secure mutual affection, carries no generative noise because, as Orit Halpern writes, there are "no degrees of freedom in selection."[7] Charles held that architecture, tasked with calculating the monumental noise of the built environment for constituents "totally unprepared for the role of free choicemaker,"[8] might do better by absorbing information to enable a more deterministic codification of its transmission.[9] As love is invoked as a difficult-to-model parameter, *Primer* argues it can be made legible through emotional subtraction. This suggests expanded communicative possibilities. Yet, as Roland Barthes explains, all declarations of love collapse to yes or no and this "poverty of terms" gives rise to an infinite variation that ascribes personal meaning.[10] In cutting away meaning for sharper transmission, the Eameses return love to its dualistic paradigm. The sensory amputation of the pods similarly enacts this logic. By structuring the message space to allow more indeterministic flow, it simultaneously renders noise more decipherable and subject to modulation. The architect is played by producers, who intervene through informational sessions, conversational guides and one-on-one confessionals about "who has the sexiest voice."[11] As head of the IBM Design Program, architect Eliot F. Noyes used *Primer* to orient employees, then brought in the Eameses to detach the computer from its wartime associations through films, exhibitions and publications.[12] They would eventually describe *Primer* as "IBM-sponsored."[13] If love is central to the management of modern societies, the Eameses correctly sutured it to the computer during the emergence of an information regime. As Halpern notes, these "discourses and methods made 'algorithm' and 'love' speakable in the same sentence."[14]

The mathematical design of communication streamlined the world as a field of channels along calculable lines. One channel is reality television. The unscripted genre descends from wartime epistemologies like *Primer*: it exemplifies simulation as a scientific tool, testing human behaviour—especially the "ordinary," the "working class," or the "real"—under engineered conflict to reveal what is lacking, dysfunctional, or in need of correction within a perceived social threat. For architect Konrad Wachsmann, the threat was the dissolution of architecture by the ambient modulations of television and his response was complete acquiescence to its grammar. Convinced society would be "designed" around the medium, he created what Mark Wigley calls a "prime-time building:" a televised program circulating and collecting architectural discourse from the populace under a controlled format that fostered emergent "impulses and improvisations" to "help society participate in its own evolution."[15] The

Above: Samiha Meem, *Love Is Blind* Pods, 2025.

prognosis was correct but his optimism is unsurprisingly revised by neoliberalism, where it functions as a precision instrument for remaking the world by teaching specific ideologies around family, religion, politics, education and even communication itself, to produce self-modulating citizens.

For *Love Is Blind*, the threat is the waning cult of heterosexuality—and the template for neutralising it, as though it were imperative, is to absorb the fully integrated, indestructible logic of information technologies. The production enforces this alongside other latent mechanisms, but most explicit is its literary overdetermination of heterosexuality, made unambiguous by the clarified computational message space.
The future unfolds backward: a proto-Edenic hut configuration that can only couple one man and one woman, who are then sent off in a single-direction flow through standardised milestones that, upon the slightest deviation, leads to the total breakdown of relationships. The emergence of dwindling biological clocks, histories of bisexuality and paltry bank balances does not arrive to

recalibrate the space of love to evolve with its constituents. Instead, it furnishes contrast with more successful couples already aligned to convention and reaffirms the rigid matrix of heterosexuality not as one option among many, but as the only one capable of coherence or reward. For the cast and audience in this prime-time building, love is small, scarce and unforgivingly exact.

Stable Pantry Problem

The wave of labour lawsuits against *Love Is Blind* by outgoing cast members—rather, 'independent contractors' working twenty-hour days for $7.14 an hour—marks the first sustained challenge to the post-Fordist framework that allows reality television to deliver content fast and at scale without paying unionised writers or actors.[16] Since this profit-squeeze prefigures the 'reality' of the show, it shapes love as a kind of work. This work is kindled by the aesthetics and processes of another flexible labour market: fulfillment centres. The Santa Clarita soundstage, provided by LA North Studios, isn't Hollywood proper but a leaner proxy: an adaptive reuse of warehouses in an industrial park shared with Costco and Amazon for economically efficient F-1 Certified studios, construction mills and ancillary services. On the first day of collective speed dating, audiences are given the God's-eye view: empty, bare-lidded, overexposed pods tiled against a matte black expanse. This scan of figures sorted into a living spreadsheet suggests not merely the liberating promise of love by order but its infinite extensibility, perhaps arrayed outward from the terminating edge of the playback window into the space of the viewer.

The live feeds arrive at an annexed corner of the soundstage, where staff monitor the action across a bank of small screens and collate information on two surfaces: a large flatscreen and a whiteboard. The flatscreen shows the daily filming schedule—colour-coded by participant, arranged by hour—tracking who occupies which pod, for how long and in what sequence. The whiteboard tracks romantic developments using magnetised headshots in tentative pairings or loose clusters.[17] For all its posture against contemporary dating technologies, these surfaces are governed by the 1962 Gale–Shapley algorithm, colloquially known as the "Stable Marriage Problem and the engine behind apps such as Hinge.[18] The formula pairs people in two-sided markets using ranked preferences: proposers approach their top choice, choosers hold their highest-ranked offer and reject the rest and the cycle repeats until proposers secure their best viable match while choosers settle for their worst. Each day, participants rank their dates and producers use the algorithm to sort them into pods. The fundamental asymmetry of the algorithm—which persists even under egalitarian revisions—delimits romantic possibilities and is further stratified by spatial disparities among pods.[19] Each conceals four to six compact robotic cameras and forty-foot-high track-mounted rigs, but five include sliding-wall cameras for high-definition close-ups. Those with higher mutual rankings occupy these "hero-cam" pods and are more likely to appear on the show.[20] The production environment behaves like its warehouse neighbours, where the spatio-temporal software—which collapses participants into machine syntax to manage accelerated conditions of desire—feeds into broader coordination across the complex to preserve the blind experience. Consequently, love registers as a question of logistics: connecting bodies, data and materials across a finite set of touchpoints within the global supply chain. Taken in sum, scattered insider accounts—journalistic expos s, legal testimonies, producer commentaries—trace this analogous operation.

The first touchpoint is sourcing. The singles are selected from audition tapes, recruited on platforms like Instagram or LinkedIn and screened through psychological evaluations to confirm their exchange value. The second, receiving, brings participants to California, where hotel rooms hold them 'on ice' before shooting begins.[21] The third, storing, brings them to the soundstage and stocks them in single-sex lounges. The fourth, processing, moves this inventory across the soundstage. As rankings roll in, the algorithm pairs and schedules. This information routes through multiple subpoints: twenty-five generic pods, five hero-cam pods, two pod-entry halls, two lounges, reveal stage, talking head station, bathrooms, the therapist and thirty hotel rooms. The pod algorithm sets the constraints necessary to eliminate traffic interference as the semi-autonomous crew 'picks' and 'packs' participants individually to and from these destinations under voice-directed coordination through the local communications network.[22] The operation pauses once daily to swap unionised workers.[23] As commitments narrow, the algorithm adjusts: reassigning locations, returning bodies to the hollow compartments of the hive. Its hierarchical subparts are arranged, like the inventory gradient in a fulfillment centre, to hold high-demand couples in hero-cam pods closer to crew stations, while lower-value participants are comparatively distant. The scale dwindles to hero-cam pods as inventory of singles thin—those who fail exit, those who succeed get engaged—until pods are removed entirely at the shipping dock of the reveal ceremony: the fifth touchpoint. A narrow carpet stretches empty between two vaults until the gates part and the engaged couple walks forward. The love containerised for the market is, at last, unboxed.

Above: Samiha Meem, *Love Is Blind*: The Reveal, 2025.

Kelly Pendergrast writes on the "logistical turn" of everyday spaces—supermarket-style pantries, walk-in closets like retail backrooms and other organised displays of accumulation—as a compulsion to forge an "intimate connection with the abstraction and depraved randomness of contemporary supply chains."[24] A click wraps the surface of the earth as it surges through acres of data centre queues, conveyor belts and shipping networks until reaching our homes in an unassuming cardboard box—while the initial gesture is quietly stored as an index of desire to modulate the mutable configuration of future stock across the network of fluid interiors. The modern dating app, too, is structured around commodity exchange. The swipe mechanism streamlines our sort through an endless supply of profiles with the machinic efficiency of an assembly line, unthinking of how they appear before us. Out of this comes the familiar paradox of abundance and scarcity, pressing our behaviour into the mold of market techniques through which we sell ourselves to locate a desirable 'object.' To stabilise our thingness in this pantry of love, algorithms collect geolocation, preferences and user behaviours to chart optimal paths—not toward a partner, but, as Illouz terms it, the "rational management of the flow of encounters."[25] And it is this flow that has replaced the literary love-lock bridges and paddle-boats-for-two as the dominant space of love in the computational machine. The platform acts as what Gilles Pach calls "invisible intermediaries" to manage circulation."[26] The producers take on this brokerage role but, rather than subverting such libidinal logistics, submit to its compulsions completely and place participants in direct contact with their own abstraction on the dating apps they so revere. The protocols ensure participants never cross paths with the opposite gender and keep them removed from the mechanics of the operation: no one knows who they will meet, when, or where until they hear a recognisable voice after being picked and packed into a pod. Otherwise, they are shelved in reserve.

Without a Terminating Edge

At the turn of the twentieth century, loosened norms of courtship and the burden of choice introduced industrialised methods to romance. The best-known example, launched in 1965 by Harvard students as Compatibility Research, was Operation Match, which sought an alternative to the 'irrationality' of the blind date

Above: Samiha Meem, Exterior of Filming Cutouts, *The New York Times*.

and mixer.[27] Questionnaires from students nationwide were sorted by proximity and other absolutes, transferred onto punch cards and processed on a pod-sized IBM 1401 to generate matches. Non-believers were told, "The Great God Computer must know something we don't," or "we're not taking the love out of love, we're making it more efficient."[28] The mixer became a sort; the blind date, a printout. This 1401 realised IBM design consultant Edgar Kaufmann Jr.'s "parlor–coal cellar" schema: the parlour as open user environment, the coal cellar as concealed technical operations. The guts of the computer are withheld for efficiency but reappear through pushbuttons, dials and panels that reach toward the user.[29] The pod enacts Kaufmann in reverse: the parlour sits within, the cellar cast outward. Each stands three feet apart to muffle sound and allow crew to tend hidden cameras. The only breach is the speaker used to communicate across the cellar. This partial knowledge lets participants focus on love while aware the cellar is covertly at their service.

Still, the cameras implicitly assert themselves in the parlour. The standard cameras operate under Orwellian field naturalism, which the editorial knife corrects through match-and-cross-cut assemblies of reaction shots and talking heads. In the early 2000s, this industry staple expanded into high-definition to accommodate the letterbox principles of cinema. The observatory mode met a more expository one: the real world needed to be more cinematic. The hero-cam pods inherit this surveillance, but their aesthetic operation rests on a spatial one. The genre often installs its subjects in two interdependent sites: the "villa," whether isolated structure or virgin landscape, commonly read as the spoils of capitalist extraction; and the "confessional," the sanctioned outlet for subjective dialogue to validate the former. The pods collapse these distinctions by doubling as secluded sites for unbridled love and as solitary seat-to-screen apparatuses reserved for the talking head. By effect, they merge the ideological subtexts of surveillance and alienation to assert human subjectivity as a commodified site: the self must be aestheticised for an unseen audience to discover real love. This, of course, the same contrived conditions of dating profiles curated and consumed to attract attention. The codes of realism hinge on what is already written and our techno-institutional complex has already abandoned the allure of the unmediated self. Even with the intent to dislodge from rituals of self-curation, participants find themselves rehearsing the same bag of tricks.

As Operation Match migrated to IBM System/360, a reimagined parlour emerged: a fish eye aerial advert positioned consumers as spectators in the limitless "radical enclosure of the white room." This heightened contrast between man and machine, John Harwood argues, "eliminat[ed] environmental stimulus" and engendered the paradoxical intimacy of being near yet removed as an enduring "icon of informational space."[30] *Love Is Blind* extols this collapsed distance but updates the white room with the logistical unit of the box: the point of exchange between global and human scales of supply and demand. The box carries not only object but swathes of information that assign value to suppliers, couriers, retailers and customers. Be it collapsible cardboard, a UI container, or a pod, the box stands in for all that is fillable and upon contact, it can square out the desire held within as a quantifiable asset. The clouded measures constructing the box beyond length, width and depth modify not just spaces or infrastructures but subjectivities and behaviours. It nurtures instant gratification disentangled from the hands that bring it into being, so love appears comfortably discovered in mediated enclosures.

This explains why the pods feel acceptable. They simulate closeness that flatters hyper- and anti-social rhythms participants already know. They summon meals to their 'cozy' cells, conduct curated dates alone and believe in intimacy in the abstract while never truly confronting the person across the cellar. The effect resembles the flow of encounters in the stack, in which the pursuit of love has become uncoupled from the pursuit of contact, yet is sustained by this very inertia. Marek Poliks and Roberto Alonso Trillo's definition of "exocapitalism" is helpful here. In the axioms of arbitrage—buy, hold, sell—the hold accrues value yet is exogenously delimited by time, labor and matter. *Primer* represents the hold in tandem with love: a vulnerable channel. Capitalism, in its bid to scale, worms into this channel. It "folds, lifts, and drags" itself away from fixed references and generates—not determines—value based on a futures market: subscription services, insurance calculations, airline miles traded wholesale. This abstraction creates limitless economies "out of nothing."[31] The hold of the stack rehearses this volatility, inflating our value against a sea of undesirables while wagering on an invisible future prospect. A date promises an exit, yet—when material worth collides with value projection—we return. The show reproduces this: connections form through speculative appraisal of self and other, only for participants to later long for the prelapsarian pod-state when the 'real world' inevitably unspools the gamble.

This dissonance toward others appeared as readily in early computer dating. Though progressive in appearance, Mar Hicks notes that Compatibility Group held conservative positions on sharing Harvard amenities with the coordinate women's college campaigning for access. The service quantified desire while dictating conditions under which women could enter male territories, defining them as products, an "IBM baby, the ideal lady," rather than equal actors.[32] Had it been built, the proposed follow-up Real-Time, where campus terminals linked to a central computer delivered on-demand dates, would have imposed a leaner logistical order.[33] Hicks describes how the computational placated anxieties over divorce rates and respectability politics by reinscribing literary ideologies of compatibility—class, race, gender, religion, nation—into a "conservative technology" shored by scientific objectivity. Operation Match, while separating love from marriage or celibacy, co-constructed gender continuities in educational spaces. Elsewhere, the 1957 Scientific Marriage Foundation encoded the church into the computer and the 1964 Com-Pat excluded social and economic differences, convinced they bred "bad marriages."[34] However limitless it appears, there are many edges to love inside the parlour.

Walled-Off Throats and Fuel-Throated Walls

The visual concept of *Love Is Blind* was *Ex Machina* meets love, which, more than a throwaway reference by production designer Dave Edwards to the 2014 science fiction film, reveals their shared technological parable. In the film, Caleb Smith, a programmer at Google stand-in Blue Book, is invited to CEO Nathan Bateman's remote facility to assess whether Ava, a robot girl, can simulate human consciousness through conversation. The evaluation hinges not on empirical reasoning but whether they might fall in love. The premise, in other words, is already romantic and near-identical to *Love Is Blind*. Caleb is immediately dislocated: first onto a remote stretch of Norwegian land, then into a labyrinthine parlour of halls and wings pulsing with electronic presence evidenced only by cameras, keypads and alarms. The sessions take place in her sparse private living area, which features a floor-to-ceiling glass observation box for Caleb with a speaking vent. As they flirt, Nathan monitors live feeds from the control room.

In *Love Is Blind*, each pod is scantily furnished—a rug, couch, side table—because, as designers note, the "focus needs to be on the wall" shared between two singles.[35] This "frozen wall" is an opaque LED surface with speakers, just above and on either side, that transduce the sound from the parallel pod in real time to give the screen a "living, breathing" presence.[36] As the observation box offers complete transparency, the opaque interface that holds Ava and Caleb apart in *Ex Machina* is her visibly inhuman skin. These prosthetic interfaces hold apart tractable bodies of data, yet also bring them together. If sound and algorithmic transmissions of the singles build an invisible joint between two pods, Caleb and Ava are bound by the mutable materialities of a networked information system that governs citizens without ever appearing. Ava is built from vast human databases moderated by Caleb, while he is selected by Nathan to evaluate her humanness based on his porn habits, socioeconomic status and psychographic pliability. As Despina Kakoudaki notes, the film stages processes of "making" and "unmaking" technologically mediated subjectivities. Ava becomes more real by extracting information from Caleb, while he questions his human status by cutting into his increasingly informatic skin.[37]As they get closer to integrating the other into themselves—perhaps this is what you call dating—the synthetic barrier dissolves and they arrive at a body–space continuum.

For the ontological crisis of the participants, the channel to make and unmake defaults to the voice. The frozen wall is, essentially, a mouth. The late nineteenth century understood the voice as the primary modality of social life and prompted sonic research and technologies to measure and reconstrue the human aural–oral apparatus that were, as Jonathan Sterne notes, advanced by "abandoning the mouth altogether."[38] This separation made the practices and boundaries of sound—inherently extrinsic, necessarily collective—subject to cultural modification as a private acoustic space that became the material condition for freedom. It steadily intervened in how we relate not just to machines and the world, but to ourselves and one another. The "digital diet," high-density foam walls and solitary exchange on *Love Is Blind* attempt to restore the so-called pure communicative space disrupted by the din of the industrial, global and urban. This is hardly new. That intimacy is embodied at the scale of the unitary body or person-to-person interaction is a millennia-long process, born from ancient philosophies of dialogue, religious dogma concerning spiritual connection and scientific literature on metabolism to support the "authoritarian preference for the one over the many."[39] This effaces institutional interference within the perpetual material exchange among the open orifices of bodies, machines and environments that make and unmake one another. Sterne details that, since the beginning of electronic media, sound technologies have been marketed to support this conception of communication and, each time they fail, produce the litany of affirmative reactions born from our indoctrinated discontent.[40] The prosthetic mouth in the pod fabricates that their love—in success or failure—is wholly on the participant. Moreover, it executes the second-order calculation Mackinnon describes as necessary to erase the technical arrangement of love by the production.

The computational discourse machine relied and built on this abstraction to, as Sarah A. Bell describes, shape the human body "as an informatic interface" through which corporate entities collect, process and communicate.[41] The logistical environment of *Love Is Blind* and *Ex Machina*—of IBM love machines, Hinge, fulfillment hubs, the hold, or the world entire—is a kind of networked throat, where it is not people or things that are exchanging intimacies but the local-and-planetary nervous system of information. It is a cold organ with a cruel sort of warmth. In the inaugural season, Jessica and Mark experience cognitive overload from fusing auditory and emotional attraction with physical connection. In a last-ditch effort, Mark arranges an at-home date with meals in separate rooms.

This return-to-simulation changes their relationship completely: Jessica softens and concludes that forced distance "brings down the walls, and you just open up." By asking if love can unmake a wall, *Love Is Blind* makes the wall the only form in which love can appear.

Above: Samiha Meem, The Frozen Wall, *Love is Blind,* Netflix.

Being Tamagotchis

Around 457 MB on my iPhone 11 is taken up by an app called Dimensional. It administers industrial-organisational personality tests to generate your psychometric "signature." This signature is built from the "many dimensions of you," and its unit of measurement is called Traits. Two hundred in all fill a colourful four-column grid that can be orbited in "360." The dashboard for a Trait shows textual and visual metrics and—most importantly—your self-score, peer-score, peer self-scores and community-scores. You can even track progress in the form of a crisp stock chart. Yes, it kind of makes you feel like a human Tamagotchi. Out of 99 percent of all users, I am higher on Introspection and lower on Trust. So, I tried to be more open. Six months later, my perfect Slow-to-Anger score had dropped 17 points. This, I suppose, is the toll exacted by other people our air-tight, occupancy-1 bubbles are designed to exclude. Now, Dimensional is expanding into matchmaking.

Their hyper-informatic platform certainly feeds the modern urge to file every human gesture into exclusionary pathologies, adaptive consumer profiles, or self-monitored optimisation for a statistical life to come, yet it reveals the very measurements by which dating apps already discreetly perceive us to orient our personal algorithms. It cracks the coal cellar open. It reminds me of how architectural practice ceded its authorial remit almost entirely to a similar information management interface. Orbiting a nominal origin, the architect observes an intelligent simulation of a precise material and affective future with an omnidirectional yet distant eye. The signature of a building is compressed into mathematical notation: a fractional tweak of a coefficient generates 'families' of objects that synchronise industry actors across the life cycle of a technical object to guarantee its error-free transmission. Every collected datum feeds forward into refining software to determine who we are and what we might do. This unified syntax narrows the space of decision until every customisation finds the same resemblance. This optimisation has always been limited to design problems and solutions that are quantifiable. As love becomes machine-readable with millimetric precision, our all-encompassing 3D file may just complete the vision of *Primer* and encode the many Traits of love within the ribbon panel on Revit to perfect its material configuration as homogenised, mass-produced and most of all, outsourced.

The question is not whether *love is blind*, but whether blindness is still a choice we will make. Perhaps we discard the temptation to see love as primal or organic and consider that true romance might be in the codes we are told to look away from. This is neither to validate Dimensional nor to accelerate the easy liberalisms, stable identities, or perfect encounters that such mathematical vision tenders. Rather, these codes are usually concealed—or inexorably exposed only to those entitled to design the sociotechnical instruments of measurement. Our obsession with enchantment serves them well: it places love entirely outside humans so that it may be discreetly inscribed with qualitative and quantitative meaning then rejoined to the material world in spurious order. To see the codes might be to ruin this trick. My seventeen-point spike in anger would otherwise direct me toward Peloton classes, a Headspace trial, or a monthly delivery of ashwagandha seltzers to make an endless hold more tolerable—or handed over to unfeeling software to lay its mark on the bricks from which, as David Greene wrote in the first issue of *Archigram*, "love [has] gone."[42] If I sound cynical or fatalistic, it is only because, despite every effort to convince myself otherwise, I still believe in love. This might be foolish.

Above: "Tuning In to Permanent Love Wave" Cartoon in Syracuse Telegram, 1923.

01 Eva Illouz, "Love, Reason, Irony," in *Why Love Hurts* (Cambridge: Polity Press, 2012), 156-197.
02 Kathryn VanArendonk, "Love Is Blind: Inside Season 7 of Chris Coelen's Experiment," *Vulture*, October 2, 2024, https://www.vulture.com/article/love-is-blind-season-7-chris-coelen-lawsuits-interview.html.
03 Lee Mackinnon, "Love Machines and the Tinder-Bot Bildungsroman," *e-flux Journal*, no. 74 (September 2016): 44–64.
04 Illouz, "Love, Reason, Irony," 156-197.
05 Mackinnon, "Love Machines."
06 Olivia Harrison, "The Design Secrets Behind the Love Is Blind Pods," *Refinery29*, February 26, 2020.
07 Orit Halpern, *Beautiful Data* (Durham, NC: Duke University Press, 2015), 106.
08 Charles Eames, *An Eames Anthology*, ed. Daniel Ostroff (New Haven: Yale University Press, 2015), 245.
09 Ibid., 136.
10 Roland Barthes, *S/Z*, trans. Richard Miller (Malden: Blackwell Publishing, 2002), 177.
11 VanArendonk, "Love Is Blind."
12 Philip Morrison and Phylis Morrison, "A Happy Octopus: Charles and Ray Learn Science and Teach It with Images," in *The Work of Charles and Ray Eames*, ed. Donald Albrecht (New York: Harry N. Abrams, 1997), 112.
13 Eames Demetrios, *An Eames Primer* (New York: Universe Publishing, 2005), 23.
14 Halpern, *Beautiful DTata*, 173.
15 Mark Wigley, "Prime Time Building," in *Konrad Wachsmann's Television* (Berlin: Sternberg Press, 2020), 323-342.
16 Emily Nussbaum, "Is 'Love Is Blind' a Toxic Workplace?" *The New Yorker*, May 27, 2024.
17 Kathryn VanArendonk, "What I Saw Inside the Love Is Blind Control Room," *Vulture*, October 24, 2024, https://www.vulture.com/article/love-is-blind-behind-the-scenes-season-7-hannah-nick-bohdan.html.
18 Julia Jacobs and Matt Stevens, "Inside the Pods With 'Love Is Blind,' the Reality TV Juggernaut," *The New York Times*, April 12, 2023, https://www.nytimes.com/2023/04/12/arts/television/love-is-blind-netflix-reality-show.html.
19 Daniel M. Gusfield and Robert W. Irving, "Elementary Concepts and Results," in *The Stable Marriage Problem* (Cambridge: MIT Press, 1989), 6–12.
20 VanArendonk, "Love Is Blind."
21 Nussbaum, "Is 'Love Is Blind' a Toxic Workplace?"
22 VanArendonk, "Love Is Blind."
23 Ibid.
24 Kelly Pendergrast, "Merchandizing the Void," *Dilettante Army*, "Wifey" (Spring 2023).
25 Illouz, "Love, Reason, Irony."
26 Gilles Paché, "Dating Apps: A 'Logistics of Desire,'" *Journal of Social Science for Policy Implications* 13 (2025): 1–8.
27 T. Jay Mathews, "Operation Match," *The Harvard Crimson*, November 3, 1965, https://www.thecrimson.com/article/1965/11/3/operation-match-pif-you-stop-to/.
28 Patsy Tarr, *Operation Match* (New York: 2wice Books, 2024).
29 John Harwood, "The Architecture of the Computer," in *The Interface: IBM and the Transformation of Corporate Design*, 1945–1976 (Minneapolis: University of Minnesota Press, 2011), 59–100.
30 Ibid.
31 Marek Poliks and Roberto Alonso Trillo, "Lift," in *Exocapitalism* (Berlin: Becoming Press, 2025), 51–92.
32 Mathews, "Operation Match."
33 Samantha Cole, *How Sex Changed the Internet and the Internet Changed Sex* (New York: Workman Publishing Company, 2022).
34 Mar Hicks, "Computer Love," *Ada: A Journal of Gender, New Media, and Technology* no. 10 (November 2016).
35 VanArendonk, "Love Is Blind."
36 Stephan Horbelt, "Pod Almighty," *Emmy Magazine*, Issue No. 8 (2024): 26–27
37 Despina Kakoudaki, "Unmaking People: The Politics of Negation in Frankenstein and Ex Machina," *Science Fiction Studies* 45, no. 2 (July 2018): 289–307.
38 Jonathan Sterne, *The Audible Past* (Durham: Duke University Press, 2003), 77.
39 Ibid., 335-351.
40 Ibid.
41 Sarah A. Bell, *Vox ex Machina* (Cambridge, MA: MIT Press, 2024): 7-23.
42 Archigram, *no. 1* (1961), Avery Architectural & Fine Arts Library, Columbia University.

LOVE IN CAPITAL LETTERS

Alex Selenitsch

There are four letters in the word LOVE. As capitals they make a sequence of a right angle, a circle (in some typefaces), an acute angle and a stem with three branches. This configuration points to complex experiences which may include states of infatuation, the bonds of community, the adoration of things, worship towards and received from divinities, the action of resolution and of reconciliation. And so on. The context of the word points to which of these experiences is being meant while the word remains the same.

What if the word was altered or written differently? Could this generate exceptional speculations or descriptions about love? These poems make such an attempt. There is no attempt to illustrate particular ideas of love; instead, there is a response to the formal properties of the letters themselves. Of these, the major one is the second letter which is easily an exclamation, a vowel and a zero and slides across all three conditions. The three poems use this circle as an armature in the same way that a circle is an armature in the international symbols for male and female.

Normally we write, print, or draw the four letters of this word in a horizontal row. It is the easiest of conventions to ignore, especially with stencilled letters which can easily slip all over a surface, be reversed, overlaid, coloured in. Stencilling encourages an additive method of composition, a kind of improvisation, with each new letter responding to what is already there and possibly without being influenced by a final result. I have done this with digital programs too, but there is a tactile reality, a direct engagement to working on paper with a cheap stencil and a pen without having to plug in or print. But only in their initial images—these poems have then been tangled up in the digital world so that they can be published, just as LOVE has always been tangled up in representations to make itself known.

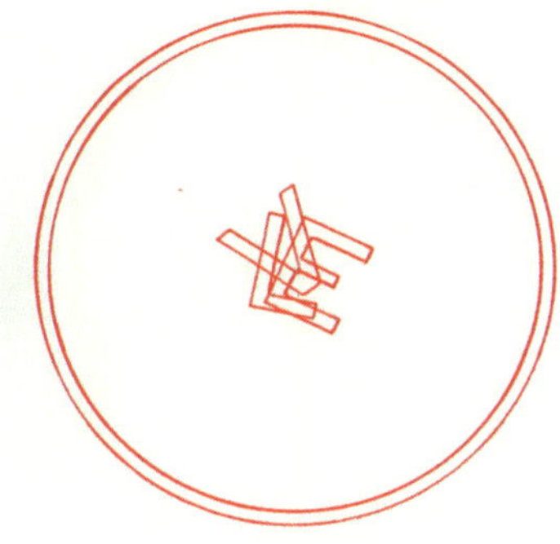

O LOVE #1
There are three letters on the circle's perimeter, like a key ring: each letter a key. Do you need one key, two keys or three keys to unlock LOVE? Maybe the keys open up other things.

O LOVE #2:
The three letters are inside the circle as if protected or as if imprisoned. Love easily slips from one condition to the other. Perhaps it's always both.

O LOVE #3:
Two of the letters have multiplied inside the perimeter and make an entangled mass, maybe a mess. Maybe a conglomerate of overlapped spontaneity. One letter dances around and touches the outside of the perimeter as security or celebration. Perhaps it's a periphery of thorns.